Howard Ben Tré

Sonja Blomdahl

Dale Chihuly

Carol Cohen

Dan Dailey

Michael M. Glancy

Sidney R. Hutter

Kreg Kallenberger

Joey Kirkpatrick and Flora C. Mace

Jon Kuhn

Dominick Labino

Marvin Lipofsky

Harvey K. Littleton

Andrew Magdanz

Dante Marioni

Richard Marquis

William Morris

Jay Musler

Joel Philip Myers

Thomas Patti

Ginny Ruffner

Mary Shaffer

Paul J. Stankard

Catherine ("Cappy") Thompson

Karla Trinkley

Steven I. Weinberg

Mary Ann ("Toots") Zynsky

Howard Ben Tré

Sonja Blomdahl

Dale Chihuly

Carol Cohen

Dan Dailey

Michael M. Glancy

Sidney R. Hutter

Kreg Kallenberger

Joey Kirkpatrick and Flora C. Mace

Jon Kuhn

Dominick Labino

Marvin Lipofsky

Harvey K. Littleton

Andrew Magdanz

Dante Marioni

Richard Marquis

William Morris

Jay Musler

Joel Philip Myers

Thomas Patti

Ginny Ruffner

Mary Shaffer

Paul J. Stankard

Catherine ("Cappy") Thompson

Karla Trinkley

Steven I. Weinberg

Mary Ann ("Toots") Zynsky

Library of Congress Catalogue Card No. 97-73290
ISBN 0-87846-447-6

Designed by Cynthia Rockwell Randall
Printed by Meridian Printing

Exhibition dates: August 13, 1997—January 11, 1998

This exhibition was organized by the Museum of Fine Arts, Boston.

The exhibition is made possible by the generous support of Beacon Properties Corporation.

Front cover:

Mary Ann ("Toots") Zynsky, *Chaos in Paradise* (no. 74, detail)

Back cover (left to right):

Sonja Blomdahl, *Peach / Ruby / Cobalt* (no. 3, detail)

Ginny Ruffner, *What Is a Style?* (no. 57, detail)

Marvin Lipofsky, with Stefan Stefko and team
IGS III Series 1988-93 #4 (no. 29, detail)

Frontispiece:

Marvin Lipofsky with master glassblower Stefan Stefko and team, Novy Bor, Czechoslovakia, 1985.

GLASS TODAY *by American Studio Artists*

Jonathan L. Fairbanks and
Pat Warner

with Linda Foss Nichols, Anne Dort Moffett,
Blake M. Morandi, Rebecca Ann Gay Reynolds,
Rozemarijn A. Verheul-Goossens, and
Gerald W. R. Ward

Museum of Fine Arts, Boston 1997

Contents

Foreword

"Glass Today by American Studio Artists" is the first exhibition to be dedicated to contemporary studio glass at the Museum of Fine Arts, Boston, and comes at a moment when great talents and extraordinary artistic imagination throughout the United States are focused on the compellingly ductile and highly versatile qualities of this material. It underlines the Museum's continuing commitment to the work of living artists in all media. Some major works by American glass artists, both past and present, are on view in our permanent galleries at all times, yet there has not been a special loan exhibition specifically about glass since "Steuben: Seventy Years of American Glassmaking" in 1976.

In 1897 Denman Waldo Ross, a trustee of the Museum, made a first modest gift to the collection of a glass tumbler, thought, at the time, to have been made by Henry William Stiegel (1729-1785) of Manheim, Pennsylvania. Thus began the American glass collection in this museum. Ross himself collected passionately in many cultural areas, and in his book entitled *A Theory of Pure Design* (1907), he articulated design concepts of harmony, balance, and rhythm that he felt were applicable to all the arts of mankind—linking in a wonderfully democratic synthesis arts that pedagogical categorization had previously rendered into hierarchical orders. Harmony, balance, and rhythm are abundant in this exhibition.

The Museum's collection of American glass continues to develop through the efforts of knowledgeable collectors, donors, and staffmembers. Many new-found friends of the contemporary glass movement in America, mentioned individually in the acknowledgments, have been instrumental in making this exhibition possible. We are particularly indebted to Dale and Doug Anderson for their enthusiasm and for essential support of this project.

Beacon Properties Corporation and one of its directors, Norman B. Leventhal, expressed great interest and enthusiasm for this project at an early stage. We are especially grateful to them for their great generosity in support of the exhibition.

The whole project would not have been possible without the work of Jonathan L. Fairbanks, the Katharine Lane Weems Curator of American Decorative Arts and Sculpture, and his dedicated staff. Pat Warner served as the exhibition coordinator, and we are enormously grateful to her. For those who seek new discoveries in translucent, reflective, or refractive sculpture, who value vivid color or prismatic brilliance, this exhibition offers many adventures.

Malcolm Rogers
Ann and Graham Gund Director

Exhibition Sponsors

Corporate Sponsor of the Exhibition
Beacon Properties Corporation

Sponsors of the Catalogue

Dale and Doug Anderson

Lisa and Dudley B. Anderson

Art Alliance for Contemporary Glass

Ann and Bruce Bachman

Lorraine and Alan Bressler

Ron and Lisa Brill

Chappell Gallery, Boston

Simona and Jerome Chazen

John and Ann Clarkeson

Bert and Rosalie Cohen

Mr. and Mrs. Norman Cohn

Alex and Camille Cook

Mr. and Mrs. Howard Davis

Leilani Lattin and William Duke

Daphne and Peter Farago

Mr. and Mrs. Solon Gershman

Daniel Greenberg and Susan Steinhauser

Carol and Charles Grossman

Stan Hatoff

Heller Gallery, New York City

Imago Galleries, Palm Desert, California

Colleen and Philip Kotelly

Nancy and Philip Kotler

Stephen and Lois Kunian

Ms. Joan Lunney

Sonia and Isaac Luski

Judy and Robbie Mann

Jeffrey and Cynthia Manocherian

Mr. and Mrs. Sidney Marx

Jane and Arthur Mason

Rita Meltzer

Metropolitan Contemporary Glass Group

Jill and Jack Pelisek

Ellen M. Poss

Dr. and Mrs. Jerome Raphael

Murray and Lois Sandler

George and Dorothy Saxe

Jon and Mary Shirley Foundation

Drs. Norman and Arlene Silvers

Mrs. Jean Sosin

Barbara and Donald Tober

David and Nancy Wolf

Lenders to the Exhibition

Many works in the exhibition were provided by the artists; we are grateful to the following individuals and institutions for their generosity in lending major works from their collections.

Dale and Doug Anderson

Mike and Annie Belkin

Lorraine and Alan Bressler

Andrea and Charles Bronfman

Capital Resource Partners

Simona and Jerome Chazen

Alfred DeCredico

Daniel Greenberg and Susan Steinhauser

The Jones Museum of Glass and Ceramics

Susan Shapiro Magdanz

Judy and Robbie Mann

Jeffrey and Cynthia Manocherian

Milwaukee Art Museum

Museum of Fine Arts, Boston

Private collection

Lois Sandler

George and Dorothy Saxe

Linda J. Schwabe and Stephen E. Elmont

6

Acknowledgments

In the spring of 1996, when the Glass Art Society met in Boston, the Department of American Decorative Arts and Sculpture at the Museum of Fine Arts, Boston, presented a small installation of contemporary glass from the Museum's collection, including works by some artists residing in New England. Susan M. Rossi-Wilcox of the Botanical Museum of Harvard University, home of the world-famous glass flowers collection, was instrumental in helping us select representative glass artists. As we prepared, I became more aware of the vastness and maturity of glass art today. Under the leadership of Jonathan Fairbanks, the Department has now, just a little more than a year later, brought together "Glass Today by American Studio Artists."

In selecting the works for this exhibition, we received advice from Gretchen Keyworth, Jody Klein, Ruth Summers, Tom Michie of the Rhode Island School of Design, Jane Adlin of the Metropolitan Museum of Art, Davira Taragin of the Toledo Museum, Jim Schantz of the Holsten Gallery in Stockbridge, and Linda Boone of Habatat Gallery, Boca Raton. Daphne Farago gave me a quick history of glass collecting which served as a foundation for subsequent research. Scott Jacobson, Lynn Leff, and Terry Davidson of Leo Kaplan Modern in New York have been exemplary in answering our many questions. The Heller Gallery, New York, has provided us with invaluable assistance as well. Douglas and Michael Heller and Bob Roberts have given all of our staff a much welcomed helping hand. Dorothy-Lee Jones, a member of the Department's Visiting Committee for twenty-five years, a collector, and the founder of the Jones Museum of Glass and Ceramics in Maine, offered essential help. Kirk Nelson of the Sandwich Glass Museum assisted us in borrowing a piece from the Glass Art Center at Bradford College in Bradford, Massachusetts. Special thanks go to Anne Jacobson and Julie Haack at the Pilchuck Glass School as well.

An undated letter fell from a copy of *Glass* last fall. It was from the Art Alliance for Contemporary Glass offering assistance to museums who would promote glass art. At about the same time happenstance brought Dale and Doug Anderson into my life just as we were debating the merits of producing a catalogue. With their encouragement and with a boost from the Art Alliance and contributions from many other individuals this catalogue became a reality. Strong friendships were formed in the process. The Andersons are connoisseurs of fine contemporary glass who have shared with us their collection and introduced us to other great collectors. Of these we are especially grateful to Dan Greenberg and Susan Steinhauser, who have not only helped with the exhibition and catalogue but also are sponsoring educational programs for young people. The Milwaukee Art Museum was most generous in lending us *Lemon/Red Crown* by Harvey K. Littleton. We would also like to express appreciation for generous assistance from Lorraine and Alan Bressler, Andrea and Charles Bronfman, Simona and Jerry Chazen, Robbie and Judy Mann, and Jeffrey and Cynthia Manocherian. Additional help has come from Susan Shapiro Magdanz, Mike and Annie Belkin, George and Dorothy Saxe, Linda J. Schwabe and Stephen E. Elmont, Lois Sandler, Alfred DeCredico, and Capital Resource Partners. With the cooperation of all, we have an exhibition of objects loaned to us by collectors, special pieces from the artists, and a catalogue to document this event.

This catalogue would not have been possible without the professional support received from members of the staff of the Department of American Decorative Arts and Sculpture, especially our prime mover Jonathan Fairbanks, Katharine Lane Weems Curator; Gerry Ward, Carolyn and Peter Lynch Associate Curator; Anne Moffett; Linda Foss Nichols; Rebecca Reynolds; Blake Morandi; and Rozemarijn Verheul-Goossens (who generously worked on the project as a volunteer). It has become an office of contemporary glass enthusiasts. I am particularly grateful to Jeannine Falino for introducing me to the Department.

Not only do we appreciate the encouragement of Ann and Graham Gund Director Malcolm Rogers, who proposed this exhibition, we also wish to thank Brent Benjamin, deputy director for curatorial affairs, and Katie Getchell, director of exhibitions and design, for smoothing the way; and William Burback, Tamsen George, Gilian Wohlauer, and Barbara Martin for their talent and input from the Department of Education and Public Programs. Dawn Griffin, Tracy Phillips, and Kelly Gifford of Public Relations have efficiently spread the word about "Glass Today." Thanks are also extended to Paul Bessire, Rebecca Rex, and Terry Lighte in the Development division for their assistance in many ways.

Our very special thanks are extended to the sponsor of "Glass Today," Beacon Properties Corporation, and to Norman B. Leventhal for the personal interest he has taken in the exhibition. The catalogue would not have been published without the contributions of many sponsors who are listed elsewhere. We especially appreciate the contributions of Dale and Doug Anderson, the Art Alliance for Contemporary Glass, Ron and Lisa Brill, John and Ann Clarkeson, Daphne and Peter Farago, Stephen and Lois Kunian, and Ellen Poss.

The production of the catalogue has been overseen with great care and lightning speed by Cynthia Purvis and Cynthia Randall of the Publications and Design Department. Tom Lang, John Woolf, and Janice

Sorkow of the Photographic Services Department have ably and swiftly supervised the photography of objects. The arrangements for collecting exhibition pieces were made by Pat Loiko, Jill Kennedy-Kernohan, and other members of the Registrar's office. Val MacGregor is owed a great round of applause for her sophisticated design in the placement of large as well as small glass objects to their best advantage. We are most grateful to Arthur Beale and the staff of the Research Laboratory, Pam Hatchfield, Will Jeffers, and Karen Gausch. Our appreciative thanks to Dave Geldart, Larry Gibbons, Max McNeil, Ray Burke, and the entire Facilities Department for their professional installation of these fragile objects.

All of the artists in the exhibition were extremely cooperative and generous in sharing information about their work. Regional artists Andy Magdanz, Dan Dailey, Howard Ben Tré, Steven Weinberg, Carol Cohen, and Michael Glancy opened their studios to us, answering our questions and offering advice, as did Sidney Hutter and Tom Patti. The community of glass artists and their collectors are a fabulous group with whom to work. We appreciate their collective enthusiasm, and their willingness in many cases to prepare objects especially for this exhibition.

Finally, I would like to thank my husband Dick who has watched me emerge from the quiet of retirement and become a full-time worker. Dinners have been late and leisurely weekends infrequent.

Pat Warner

Introduction

This exhibition of works by twenty-eight artists is characterized by contrasts. It represents a vibrant cross section of a now mature generation of American glass artists whose works range in scale from the monumental to the minute, and in mood from quiet eloquence to brash robustness. The fluid grace of hot blown glass contrasts with more architectonic constructions made from cast or cold plate glass. Subject matter ranges from personal narrative and fantasy to expressive abstractions.

There are limits, of course, to the range of items selected. Not included are stained glass; glass jewelry; glass as fiber art for fashion, prism making, and tablewares; and glass for industrial, laboratory, and space-age products. These areas of glassmaking have their own history, intrinsic beauty, and design merits, which fall beyond the focus of this exhibition. Also excluded are works by many important artists who have contributed greatly to American studio glass art. The influential Italian glass artist Lino Tagliapietra (b. 1934), for example, has been a powerful collaborator and presence in this country. Along with Livo Seguso (b. 1930) and others, he introduced long-guarded secrets of Venetian glass arts into the bloodstream of American glassmaking. While glasswork today is international in scope, this exhibition is selected from artists whose careers developed at least initially in the continental United States.

All artists in this exhibition work in three-dimensional or sculptural ways. They are concerned with issues of solids and voids, envelopes, layers, color veils, profiles or silhouettes, and illusions of space as well as compositional groupings arranged in solid occupation of space. Almost every artist gained his or her early training in college. They draw upon experience as painters, draftsmen, ceramists, designers, and modelers in order to discover their "voice" in a medium that has only been available in America on a scale suitable for a studio for about thirty-five years. Although the story of this development has been published elsewhere, it might prove instructive for Museum visitors to briefly recall this recent history.

In the late nineteenth century, art glass was dominated by the masters, John LaFarge (1835-1910) and Louis Comfort Tiffany (1848-1933). Frederick Carder (1863-1963) came to this country in 1903, having worked as art director with the Stephens and Williams Company of Stourbridge, England. In America he was the principal artistic talent to found the Steuben Glass Works in Corning, New York. That company was acquired by the Corning Glass Works as its Steuben Division in 1918. With changes in management Carder was sidelined in 1933 as a design force in the company. Yet for the rest of his life he maintained a small furnace in his studio at the plant for experimental work on his own. In the 1930s, Steuben glass took on the now familiar look of the tableware sculpture and engraved crystal so brilliantly marketed to popular taste ever since. Similar decorative colorless glass, skillfully made in large factories, existed not only at Corning, but also in Toledo, Ohio, at the Libbey Glass Company, and at Fostoria in West Virginia, where excellence of workmanship transcended artistic experimentalism. Other factories in West Virginia, such as Morgantown, Blenko, and Fenton, also produced quality art glass and tableware for popular sale.

The vast mechanization that followed the Second World War seemed to drain much of the country's creative energy into engineering methods for mass-manufactured products. Americans fell in love with the machine and the factory, and with inexpensive, attractive, and standardized consumer goods produced for the middle-class market. There were, of course, a few artists, independent and reactionary, who set out to develop personal expressions with their chosen medium in studios rather than factory environments.

One such individual was Maurice Heaton (1900-1990) of Valley Cottage, New York. Heaton's family background was in the glassmaking industry, but he approached his work with originality. He developed unique tools and molds to slump and alter plate glass, which he shaped and polished before heat fusing it with powdered colors and enamels.

Another independent explorer was the English immigrant John Burton (1894-1985) of Santa Barbara, California. He mastered the art of lampworking in intricate patterns of lively colors and ingenious configurations. Infused with his personal enthusiasm, his glass vividly reflects a broad philosophical approach. Through demonstrations, lectures, and publications, he explained to rapt audiences that the key to correcting mankind's many social disorders was to be found in art. In 1958, he had an exhibition at the Seattle Art Museum, one of the earliest solo art exhibitions for a studio glass artist.

A third pioneer was Edris Eckhardt (b. 1910) of Cleveland, Ohio. She appears to be the first American studio glass artist to formulate her own glass batches, and is the first woman artist in this country to work glass sculpturally. Her impulse to work in glass came about in 1953 during a visit to the Museum of Fine Arts, Boston. A successful potter, she was intrigued with the Museum's display of gold-colored ancient glass, and decided to rediscover the process. In 1968, she became the first living studio artist to enjoy a solo exhibition at the Corning Museum of Glass. A handsome and early work by Eckhardt, *St. Elmo* (1959), references her initial inspiration by works of art in this Museum. It seems poetic that *St. Elmo* should come back here for viewing, on loan from the Glass Center, Bradford College, although not on view in this exhibition. Instead, it appropriately joins works by other American glass pioneers and contemporary glass artists in a complementary installation in our Contemporary Crafts Gallery.

If Eckhardt, Heaton, and Burton swam against the mainstream of glass as manufactured product, two other artists whose works are displayed in this exhibition turned the tide itself. In 1962, Harvey K. Littleton set up a small pot furnace on the grounds of the Toledo Museum of Art (with the encouragement of the Museum's director, Otto Wittmann) and gathered eight artist/craftsmen in an effort to produce blown glass on a scale compatible with an artist's studio. The first melt was not a success, and Littleton called on his friend, Dominick Labino of Grand Rapids, Ohio, who had long worked in glass research for the Johns-Manville Corporation. Labino converted the furnace into a small day tank and supplied it with no. 475 marbles—a glass formula with low-melting properties that he had developed to produce fiberglass. That melt was a success, and word spread that a long-regarded industrial trade had crossed over into the world of studio art. This was but a step away from introducing hot glass art into university curricula—a step taken by Littleton at the University of Wisconsin and subsequently by many of his students at other universities. Within eight years more than fifty schools in America had hot glass studios up and running.

Labino trained as an engineer at the Carnegie Institute of Technology and his design sense was nourished at Toledo Museum's Art School. His world embraced science, history, art, technology, and studio practice. His association with the glass industry spanned fifty years. In 1965, when he retired from Johns-Manville as a vice president and director of research and development, he held more than fifty patents in America and more than twice as many abroad. Not only glass products, but also the machines for forming glass fibers (so essential to space travel) were among his achievements. In 1952 he invented a pure silica fiber that in 1980 was used to make the protective tile shields for the spacecraft *Columbia*.

Retirement from industrial work did not dampen Labino's creativity. In 1973 he made six glass bells to reconstruct an early nineteenth-century glass harmonica for the Museum of Fine Arts, Boston. Clearly, Labino was a Renaissance man who could move deftly from invention through technical fabrication to artistic expression. He was not only an artist but also an educator, and enjoyed freely sharing knowledge. His innumerable seminars and workshops played a major part in the studio glass movement. Although the works displayed here are small, Labino did create many large-scale compositions; perhaps the best known of these is his 88 by 104 in. polychrome glass mural of cast panels, *Vitrana,* made in 1969 and displayed at the Toledo Museum of Art.

Dominick Labino and his wife, Elizabeth

Dominick Labino is represented in this exhibition by an inverted drop-shaped form (no. 27) made in 1970 and given to the Museum of Fine Arts in 1983 by friends of Labino, Mr. and Mrs. James A. Saks. The work is descriptively entitled *Emergence in Polychrome with Gold and Silver Veiling*. It exhibits Labino's mastery of form and color in a subtle marriage of both technical perfection and artistic sensitivity. Another work by Labino (no. 28), on loan from the Jones Museum of Glass and Ceramics, was made in 1975. It is core-formed, a process of shaping and decorating glass employed by Egyptians in the Eighteenth Dynasty about 1400 B.C. Labino's interest in early glass technology prompted his experimentation and research through the replication of process.

Harvey K. Littleton's search for a vehicle to develop studio glass potential intersected with Labino's extraordinary technical knowledge at a propitious moment. Born in Corning, New York, the son of the director of research at the Corning Glass Works, Littleton was a friend of Frederick Carder. After beginning his formal artistic training in art classes at Elmira College, he studied physics at the University of Michigan. He shifted to the Cranbrook Academy of Art for a spring semester, before returning to the University of Michigan to study industrial design. Military service in the United States Army Signal Corps took him to Africa, Italy, and France. After discharge in 1945 he attended Brighton School of Art, England, where he modeled a torso that he cast in multiform glass at the Corning Glass Works. Returning to Michigan to study industrial design, he received a Bachelor of Design degree in 1947. While in Ann Arbor, he studied with this writer's father, the sculptor Avard T. Fairbanks (1897-1987), a proponent of the theory of dynamic symmetry—the idea that static form could be made to express motion by means of torquing and tilting the form, with the result of contrasting short versus long linear gestures.

After graduation, Littleton's career branched into pottery and design. For a time he taught pottery in Ann Arbor and subsequently at Toledo Museum's Art School. There he founded the Toledo Potters' Guild. In 1951 he returned to Cranbrook and worked with the eminent potter Maija Grotell (1899-1973) and received a master of fine arts degree. In 1951, Littleton joined the faculty of the department of art at the University of Wisconsin, Madison, where he stayed until 1977. There he first made his reputation as an

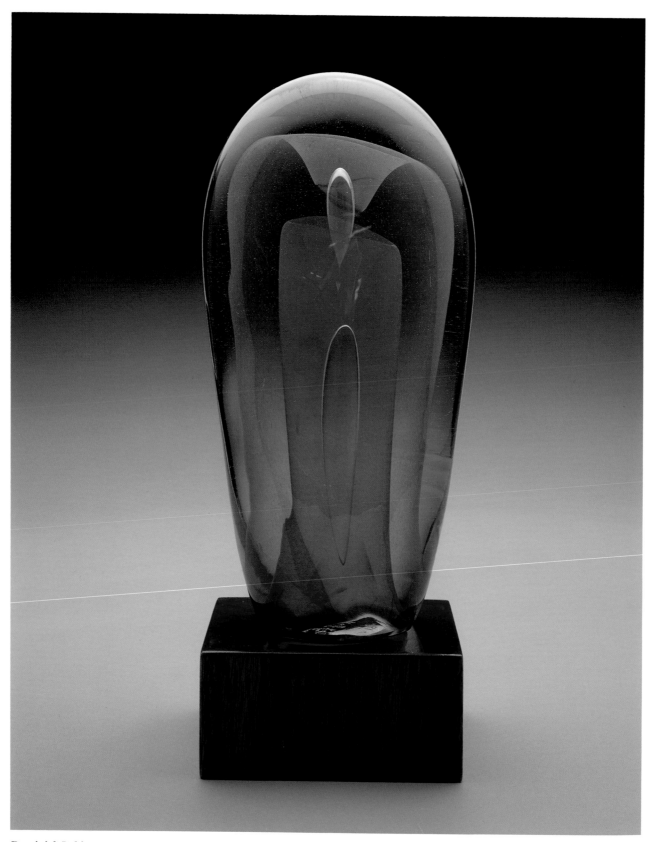

Dominick Labino
Emergence in Polychrome with Gold and Silver Veiling, 1970 (no. 27)
Museum of Fine Arts, Boston

14

artist-potter and by 1959 was elected a trustee of the American Crafts Council. In 1958, he returned to glass by melting it in his ceramic kiln in Verona, Wisconsin. Three years later he presented a paper at the fourth national conference of the American Crafts Council entitled "A Potter's Experience with Glass." In 1962 the two famous seminar workshops in glassblowing at the Toledo Museum of Art took place. Also in that year Littleton met glass artist Erwin Eisch (b. 1927) in Frauenau, West Germany. Eisch became not only a friend but a seminal influence in Littleton's expressive approach to glassworking. The remainder of Littleton's career has been devoted to glass—to expanding its influence and investigating new ways to make artistic use of this substance.

In 1984, this writer had an occasion to visit with Littleton in Washington, D.C., while reviewing craftsmen grants for the National Endowment for the Arts. Littleton was already a legendary figure in studio glass arts. That year the Renwick Gallery of the National Museum of American Art displayed his major retrospective exhibition organized by the High Museum of Art in Atlanta. This writer enjoyed touring that exhibition with Littleton. It was clear then, as it is today, that Littleton is a restless, organizing spirit, exploring, probing, and testing new exciting possibilities for art. He currently is working in Spruce Pine, North Carolina, producing intaglio prints called vitreographs, made from glass plates, a process he developed in 1974.

Littleton poetically explained the mystery and beauty captured in the process of glassmaking in 1989: "lunar brilliance grows as solar heat fades and form emerges." By contrasting cold (lunar) with hot (solar) and noting the moment when the supercooled liquid called glass takes on the shape and surface it assumes at room temperature, Littleton grasps the essence of experience. Eloquent form that traps brilliant color is Littleton's extraordinary achievement, as in his *Lemon / Red Crown* in this exhibition (no. 31). Additionally, he is a persuasive organizer and great teacher. For these contributions, his career is honored with innumerable awards, degrees, and publications. In 1983 he was awarded the Gold Medal of the American Crafts Council, the highest honor given by that organization. Works by the artist are owned and displayed at major museums throughout the world.

After Labino and Littleton moved glass into the artist's studio and into college curricula, exhibitions proliferated from California to New York City. Glass collecting, periodicals, and societies emerged and matured. The Toledo Museum and the Corning Glass Museum assumed leadership roles for national invitationals. This period is well tracked by Susanne K. Frantz in her essay, "The Evolution of Studio Glass Collecting and Documentation in the United States," in *Contemporary Crafts and the Saxe Collection*, the superb catalogue of an extraordinary exhibition organized by Davira S. Taragin for the Toledo Museum in 1993. The Montreal Exposition of 1967 displayed spectacular glass sculpture in the Czechoslovakian Pavilion by Stanislav Libensky and Jaroslavá Byrchtova. Littleton's student, Dale Chihuly, declared it to be the most impressive thing he had ever seen. Within two years a second watershed took place with the opening of the exhibition "Objects: USA." The time was ripe for Littleton's students, a new wave of glass artists, to dramatically enlarge and change the character of the field.

Harvey K. Littleton

It is impossible to survey briefly the explosion of studio glassmaking over three decades. But this exhibition offers evidence of extraordinary educational connections, both formal and informal, between most of the artists whose works are included. All but Steven I. Weinberg, Carol Cohen, Jon Kuhn, Joel Philip Myers, Thomas Patti, and Kreg Kallenberger share a lineal educational descent that begins with Littleton and his students. In the mid to late 1960s, Marvin Lipofsky and Dale Chihuly studied with Littleton. In the early 1970s, Andrew Magdanz was an assistant in Littleton's Wisconsin studio and attended his classes. In 1978 he moved to California and studied with Lipofsky at the California College of Arts and Crafts in Oakland. Jay Musler had been there in the early 1970s.

Chihuly's meteoric career touched almost everyone who cared about studio glass. Without question he has been its most ardent and successful artist/advocate/promoter. With a master of science degree from Wisconsin, he moved on to obtain a master of arts degree from the Rhode Island School of Design in 1968. The following year, on a Fulbright grant, he worked in Murano (Venice) at the Venini glass factory—the first American to do so. Three years later, while a visiting artist at RISD, he founded a center for glassworking with the support of John H. and Anne Gould Hauberg on a tree farm north of Seattle. Chihuly's summer experience at the Haystack School, Deer Isle, Maine, served as his model for the new Pilchuck Glass School. Chihuly's extraordinary creativity attracted students, faculty, collectors, and patrons sharing an irrepressible vision for glass. The story of the Pilchuck School, handsomely illustrated with pho-

Harvey K. Littleton
Lemon / Red Crown, 1989 (no. 31)
Milwaukee Art Museum

tographs of many artists whose works are in this exhibition, has recently been written by Tina Oldknow in *Pilchuck: A Glass School* (1996).

The Rhode Island School of Design produced other major glass artists represented in this exhibition. Dan Dailey and Toots Zynsky, for example, studied in the program during Chihuly's tenure. After Dailey received his master of fine arts degree, he organized the glass program for the Massachusetts College of Art, Boston, in 1974. There, Sidney R. Hutter became one of his students after working with Joel Philip Myers at Illinois State College. Sonja Blomdahl was another student of Dailey's at Mass Art.

The 1980s were seminal years for most artists represented in this exhibition. During this time their conceptual vision matured and diversified. Michael Glancy, Karla Trinkley, Howard Ben Tré, and Steven Weinberg received their graduate degrees from RISD in 1980 or shortly thereafter. A year before, Chihuly invited Lino Tagliapietra to America to collaborate with glassblowers and share the mysteries of Venetian art. Tagliapietra, Dante Marioni, Flora C. Mace, Dan Dailey, and Richard Marquis have all taught at the Haystack School. Penland has hosted visiting artists Paul J. Stankard, Ginny Ruffner, Richard Marquis, Thomas Patti, and Littleton. What seems most remarkable is the fact that despite the many close connections between artists, each individual's work remains recognizably unique, not only in technique but also in expressive voice.

Almost every movement in contemporary art is reflected or anticipated by studio glass art made in America. Littleton's earliest free-blown works show kinship to the Zen qualities of abstract expressionism. Marvin Lipofsky continued to explore and develop those aspects of freedom from precise control. Pop and funk art movements of the 1960s are referenced by the works of Richard Marquis. Joel Philip Myers's discoveries seem to be connected to color-field painting. Minimalism is reflected in the work of Howard Ben Tré. Dan Dailey connects with deconstructivism while referencing the art deco that permeates post-modernism. Although Sonja Blomdahl produces functional vessels, in reality her work has no preponderant utility other than to please the eye and celebrate the memory of vessel use. The role of conceptual art is seen in the work of Sidney R. Hutter, Karla Trinkley, Tom Patti, and other artists in the exhibition. Illusion, narrative, and fantasy are referenced by Mary Shaffer, Cappy Thompson, and Paul Stankard.

This exhibition offers a sampler—or a record of a moment in time after which the world of glass art in this country will change dramatically. Dale and Doug Anderson, who are the major lenders to this exhibition, made this observation and thereby urged and supported in part the publication of this record. They have collected glass for some twenty-five years, during which time they've witnessed amazing changes in the glass movement in this country. They feel that now all major artists in the field have come to a critical plateau in their professional maturity. Working methods are well resolved. Major technical hurdles are solved. Now seems to be the moment of dynamic potential.

Jonathan L. Fairbanks

F.A.C.C. (Hon.)

Katharine Lane Weems Curator of American Decorative Arts and Sculpture

Note to the Reader

The following catalogue contains brief essays on the work of twenty-six artists. Although the works of the pioneering glass artists Harvey K. Littleton and Dominick Labino are included in the exhibition, they are discussed in the Introduction rather than in separate entries. Several works by each artist are on display, but only one object by each artist is illustrated. Each illustration is accompanied by a short-title caption; more complete information, including materials, dimensions, and full credit lines, is provided in the checklist. Background information and documentation for each entry is contained in the sources listed for each artist in the Selected Bibliography and in the Museum's maker and object data files. The author of each entry is indicated by his or her initials.

Howard Ben Tré

Distinguished for the monolithic purity of form of his cast-glass sculpture, Howard Ben Tré is best known in Boston for his impressive fountain, *Immanent Circumstance,* located at Post Office Square and completed in 1992. Described as "the best new piece of sculpture in the city," that work combines cast Pyrex, bronze, stone, brick, and granite pavers with water in a dynamic synthesis of artistic imagination and engineering insight. This writer had the good fortune to visit the artist's studio when he was designing the ring and arc of the water jets. The intent was to produce a dome of water above the columns. The problem was how to make the jets intersect precisely at an oculus in the center of the dome to create a columnar fall of water in the fountain's center. The result speaks for itself; the water dome works and the falling water column completes the implicit relationship between what seems to be the frozen, solid, green glass of the columns and the fluidity of the water. Ben Tré's use of pitted, matte, translucent glass in a formal arrangement of columns cannot but reference the classical past, yet the whole remains clearly contemporary in its vocabulary of mixed materials.

The pair of benches in this exhibition (no. 1) are furniture only in the sense that they could serve as seating forms. But they suggest a reversible geometry that is essential to sculpture meant to convey a sense of movement. Light filters through the glass to create a sense of mass and density within. Yet the semi-matte surface denies full visual penetration—it is as if the viewer is looking at or into an ice-covered lake. Gold leaf on the metallic bonded sides reflects warm light in contrast to the cool tint of the glass itself. Dentils at each end of each bench suggest ancient architecture or frag-ments salvaged from the classical past. Yet these benches are clearly new. Such ambiguities challenge the viewer's search for the essential meanings of the forms.

Ben Tré is especially well known for his columns of glass (no. 2). Although these are not site specific, their presence is profoundly affected by and reciprocally affects the space they occupy. The artist begins with gesture drawings in notebooks, followed by full-scale drawings. Then he constructs Styrofoam models from which molds are taken in founder's resin-bonded sand. (The process is similar to sand-casting bronze sculpture.) The Styrofoam is removed and the sand molds are filled with molten glass in a factory. The object is cooled in an annealing oven for several weeks to prevent fracture or stress. Back in the studio, the surface is cut and ground to perfect the form. Sandblasting, metallic or stone work, and coloring follows. Metal powders, layers of leaf, and pigmented waxes are applied to simulate natural patina. Ben Tré's sculptures possess a serenity and nobility that minimizes the risky and arduous process of their creation. There is a figural humanity in his work, suggesting a timelessness inherent in the universal language of art.

Ben Tré holds degrees from the Rhode Island School of Design and Portland State University, Oregon. His grant, award, and exhibition record is extensive, and his works are in more than fifty museums and in many private collections.

JLF

Howard Ben Tré
Bench 8 and 9, 1988 (no. 1)
Private collection

Sonja Blomdahl

Since receiving her B.F.A. from the Massachusetts College of Art, Boston, in 1974, Sonja Blomdahl has mastered the art of glassblowing largely on her own. Although Dan Dailey (q.v.) started the glass department at Mass Art during Blomdahl's senior year, providing her with her first opportunity to try glass, her degree was in ceramics. After graduation, she ran a small glass studio with several friends in western Massachusetts, making tourist items. Determined to master glassblowing at a higher level, Blomdahl worked for six months at the Orrefors factory in Sweden. After serving as a teaching assistant to Dan Dailey at the Pilchuck Glass School in Stanwood, Washington, she moved from her native Massachusetts to Seattle, where she worked for other glass artists and spent the summers teaching at Pilchuck. There, in 1978, she had the opportunity to study with the visiting Venetian glass master, Checco Ongaro, who taught her the *incalmo* or the double-bubble technique, for which she is now known.

Color and symmetry define Sonja Blomdahl's work. Using Ongaro's technique, she blows two separate bubbles of different colored glass, linking them together with a clear band. By layering one color over another she can achieve a total of four colors, two in each half of the sphere, attaching the two bubbles to create a vessel. Her earlier vessel forms, like *Pink / Clear / Blue* (no. 4), evoked landscapes. When the light strikes the connecting band just right, the band serves as the horizon line between earth and sky.

Peach / Ruby / Cobalt (no. 3) is a dramatic manipulation of shape and color. Ever mindful of her personal need for symmetry, Blomdahl has elongated the earlier spheres into taller, narrow-neck vessel forms with inturned top openings. Here she has replaced her earlier clear band with a glorious ruby red that reflects the complex hues from both above and below. The play of transmitted and reflected light provides an ever-changing colorscape as the viewer's perspective changes.

Sonja Blomdahl's work is in the collection of the American Craft Museum, the Corning Museum of Glass, and the Renwick Gallery of American Art, among many others.

PW

Sonja Blomdahl
Peach / Ruby / Cobalt, 1996 (no. 3)
Collection of the artist

Dale Chihuly

Chartreuse Macchia with Oxblood and Ivy Green Jimmies, Opaline Spined Sea Form with Cadmium Yellow Persians, Lavender Macchia Set with Deep Red Lip Wraps: the titles of Dale Chihuly's trademark forms underscore his intense preoccupation with color and light. Chihuly's love affair with glass began by chance when, as an undergraduate interior design major, he incorporated glass into a weaving assignment at the University of Washington. Chihuly became an early graduate student in Harvey K. Littleton's (q.v.) glass program at the University of Wisconsin. A quick learner, he left after only nine months to earn his M.F.A. and to help establish a glass program at the Rhode Island School of Design in 1968. After graduating, he became the first American artist known to have worked in an Italian glass factory, traveling on a Fulbright grant to the Venini Glass Factory on Murano, Venice.

As co-founder and current artistic director of Pilchuck Glass School in Stanwood, Washington, Chihuly brings together the best glass craftspeople to teach more than 250 students annually. His work represents the collaborative efforts of large teams of artists, architects, and apprentices, an approach that not only suits his personality and style, but also proved practical after he lost his left eye in an automobile accident in 1976, and with it his depth perception. In this collegial and energetic atmosphere, Chihuly's orchestrations embody contemporary art's concern with process, risk-taking, and discovery.

The aesthetic issues that infuse Chihuly's work are inherent to the medium itself: the materialization of light, transparency, the embodiment of color, and the mutability of form. Another defining characteristic of Chihuly's work is a desire to capture the formative moment when creation occurs and

is still fluid. Drawing on the rhythms of nature, Chihuly has produced such series as the Sea Forms, Persians, and the Macchia ("spotted") pieces. In these works, color becomes form as colored light emanates from the pieces and extends into the environment. Chihuly's early blanket cylinders, inspired by a Navajo blanket exhibition that Chihuly attended at the Museum of Fine Arts, Boston, in 1975, evidence a comparatively staid presence. These simple vessels are constructed from a gather of glass to which a pattern of threads of richly colored glass are fused and then blown into cylindrical form. The two pieces in this exhibition (nos. 6, 7) represent recent attempts to carry this idea further.

Chihuly is probably the most internationally acclaimed glass artist working today. During the Venezia Aperto Vetro, the first Biennale of Glass, in 1996, he and his international team created fourteen spectacular installations, including chandeliers which were hung over the canals, in alleyways, and at the ducal palace in Venice, Italy. Chihuly has taught and worked with many artists represented in this show. The record of his exhibitions, his awards, and the collections that hold his work is extensive.

RAGR

Dale Chihuly
Blue Soft Cylinder with Green Lip Wrap, 1996 (no. 7)
Collection of Dale and Doug Anderson

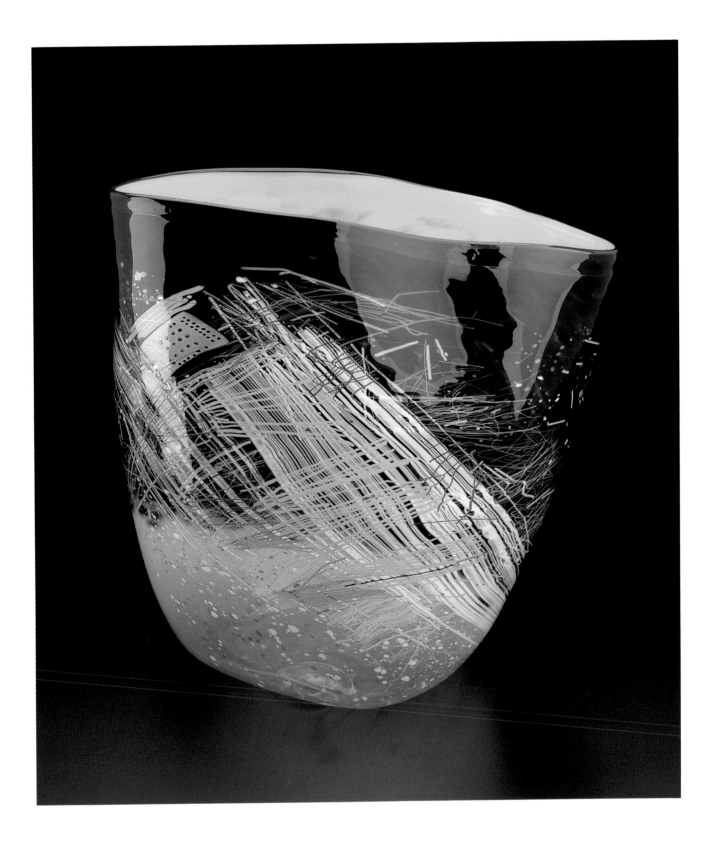

Carol Cohen

Carol Cohen's painterly constructions draw upon the peculiar properties of glass to reflect or to enclose space. The artist explores the illusion of space by feathery or pointillistic strokes of color on regularly spaced glass plates. The epoxy resin paint is permanently bonded to the glass, and each sheet of glass contains only a portion of the subject. When assembled, the separate strokes of paint create an illusion of three-dimensional form (surprisingly like that of a hologram). Seen edgewise, the image dissolves and the viewer is left looking at an assembly of plates and its frame support. Cohen sometimes constructs and paints the supporting structure, as in *Greek Revival* (no. 8). Although the subject matter and form of the frame may have nothing directly to do with the image within, implicit connections associate the exterior with the interior. In this instance, the exterior/interior dialogue relates to Cohen's travel to the Greek isles. The light greenish cast of the glass sheets creates a sense that the images hover within a water-like or gel medium. This enhances the paradox of the viewer's seeing a form that is known not to really exist.

In the artist's sunny, industrial-style studio in Cambridge, Massachusetts, ideas are suggested by materials scattered about, being tested. Partially finished works, sketches, and notes on tests jostle for space with modular sections of glass and wire-mesh fencing about to be assembled. Live plants in various stages of bloom face a wall of glass. Industrial equipment (welding apparatus, kilns, and so forth) is in another room. Cohen designed and built a spatial locater (shown in the illustration above), which points precisely to her imaginary stations for brushmarks—a painterly strategy akin to laying out sections of a topographic map. Such disparate elements all somehow seem to cohere to assist the artist's search for the potential "subject within."

The large figural composition exhibited here, *Little Compton* (no. 9), was undertaken specifically for this exhibition. It represents a response to the challenge of scale offered by the Museum's Foster Gallery.

Cohen studied painting and design at the Carnegie Institute of Technology, Pittsburgh. She holds an A.B. degree (1961) in anthropology and sociology from George Washington University. Her publication, award, honor, and exhibition record is extensive. Her works are in public museums from Japan to Switzerland; her public art on view in Boston includes a steel wall-sculpture in the Sheraton Hotel.

JLF

Carol Cohen
Greek Revival, 1994 (no. 8)
Museum of Fine Arts, Boston

Dan Dailey

Dan Dailey's youthful aspiration to be a cartoonist is evident in his economy of expression and in the keen wit that permeates his work. Though his craftsmanship is superb, the materials and techniques of its fabrication are not the basis of Dailey's inspiration. He generates his ideas through constant sketching, a habit he attributes to his father, who was an industrial designer. Dailey incorporates factory work with his personal studio work as he coordinates teams of artists and skilled technicians at every step in the creative process, from blowing, to sandblasting, acid polishing, and enameling.

Dailey's work is consciously stylized in form, often possessing an art deco geometry or 1950s futuristic aesthetic. Despite the humor of his pieces, Dailey's historical references to classic forms and his meticulous execution reflect the underlying seriousness of his work. He aims to capture the essence of his characters and to design his vessels in a way that is more than decorative. The ostensibly utilitarian works in his Animal Vessel series compare to work by native cultures such as Northwest Coast Indians, in which each sculpture is as much an animal as a vase.

While Dailey has been engaged with the production of lamps, tabletop sculptures, and even architectural commissions such as a cast wall in New York City's Rainbow Room at Rockefeller Center, it is the vessel form that most captivates him. He began fabricating vessels in 1968, and such vase series as Travel, Science Fiction, Face, and Circus have dominated his oeuvre ever since. Each piece is identified with a traditional name such as *Baboon* (no. 14), as well as a combination of letters and numbers representing the acronym for the particular series, in this case "AV" or Animal Vase, followed by its number in the series and the year of fabrication, "25–94."

Dailey received his B.A. from the Philadelphia College of Art, and his M.A. from Rhode Island School of Design while Dale Chihuly (q.v.) headed the glass department there. Following his graduate experience, Dailey went to work at the Venini glass factory in Murano, Italy, where he witnessed the industrial potentials of his medium. As an industrial designer, Dailey has developed relationships with Cristallerie Daum, Fenton Art Glass, Steuben Glass, and the Herman Miller Company. He has taught at numerous institutions including the Massachusetts Institute of Technology, the Rhode Island School of Design, Pilchuck Glass School, and Haystack Mountain School of Crafts. He also founded the glass program at Massachusetts College of Art. The recipient of many awards and fellowships, Dailey has exhibited his work at galleries and museums throughout the world.

RAGR

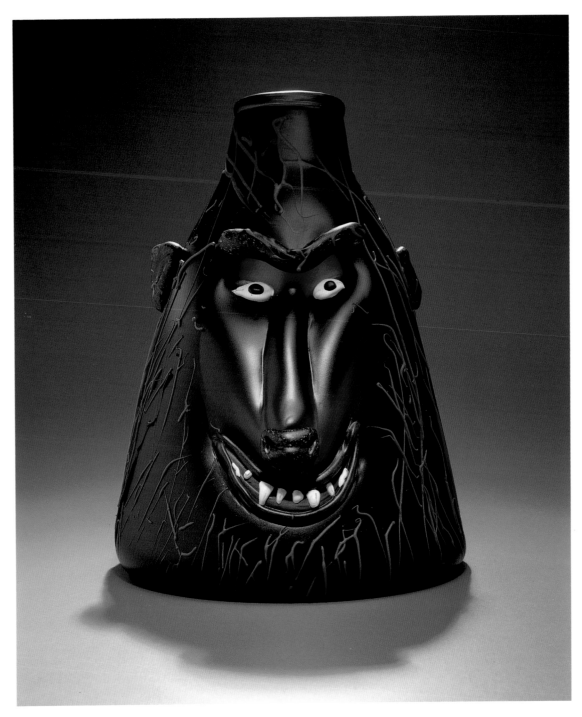

Dan Dailey
Baboon, 1994 (no. 14)
Collection of George and Dorothy Saxe

Michael M. Glancy

In a small room within the metals studios at the Rhode Island School of Design, Michael Glancy encases his blown and sandblasted glass forms with copper electroforming. Anodes, clamped onto crisscrossing rods, dangle in the blue water, and as the glass that is the cathode emerges from its bath, Glancy appears as the midwife at a primordial birth.

While an undergraduate at RISD, Glancy happened upon the closet-like lab that he still uses today. *Incognito Ruby Guardian* (no. 15), *UV Expansion* (no. 16), and *Magna Eclipsed* (no. 17), are but three of the works Glancy has cre-

ated since 1978, when he began to use the electroforming technique. Briefly, a liquid bath suspends particles of metal that are deposited on another metal (electroplating) or non-metallic form or mold (electroforming) by means of electrical current; the anode is attached to a positive wire, and the cathode, which is the object, is attached to a negative wire.

Yearly, Glancy travels to Sweden in order to orchestrate the blowing of his blanks with the master glassblower Jan-Erik Ritzman. At home in his Rehoboth studio Glancy employs cold-work techniques to create his compositions. After sandblasting a web-work that embraces the form, Glancy sprays relief areas with electrically conductive paint in preparation for the electroforming bath. The resulting copper maze is then patinated.

Glancy's imagination is aroused by looking at the physical structure of things under a microscope, by understanding the nature of a living substance. Glancy applies mathematical relationships to the microscopic elements that have sparked his creativity. In lesser hands, this obsession with structure and mathematics might translate into works of cold, mathematical precision. But *UV Expansion* is an intensely sensual expression of Glancy's mental agility and love of theoretical concepts. The liquid purple and pink form overflows the electroformed furrows that attempt to encase the vessel, and overtakes the plates, which define the composition. The expansion seems infinite, although invisible. A lens cut into the body of the vessel asserts Glancy's fascination with looking into the structure of things.

It is art that Glancy is after, and as with the science of molecular biology, irregularity and regularity combine to describe truth or beauty. When James D. Watson and Francis H. C. Crick presented their discovery of the symmetry-breaking structure of DNA in model form to a collegue, it was said, "the structure is too pretty not to be true." Within Glancy's work elegant form and linear expression flirt with chaos.

LFN

Michael M. Glancy
UV Expansion, 1994 (no. 16)
Collection of Daniel Greenberg and Susan Steinhauser

Sidney R. Hutter

Sidney R. Hutter, an artist from Waltham, Massachusetts, uses the vessel as an icon. It is the vessel's form, as opposed to its function, that interests him. During his undergraduate work at Illinois State University he visited the glass school at Pilchuck in 1975. Four years later, while working toward

his M.F.A. in glass and sculpture at the Massachusetts College of Art in Boston, Hutter started experimenting with commercial plate glass to create the image of traditional vessels. A course at the Lowell Institute of M.I.T. helped him draft accurate working drawings.

Hutter's experiences with glassblowing and his interests in design, drafting, and architecture led him to depict a three-dimensional object using two-dimensional components. After almost twenty years Sidney Hutter is still pursuing, redefining, and nurturing his original concept.

Hutter's first step is to decide on the shape of the vessel: its edge profile. An accurate drawing specifies the size of each element that will go into the final sculpture. The sheets of glass are cut, ground, and polished using machines created solely for the purpose of creating these works. Finally, all components are carefully cleaned and hand-laminated, using ultraviolet light, which cures the glue. Hutter dyes the glue to add color to his transparent vessels. Most of his techniques come out of the plate-glass industry. As the artist puts it, "I'm an industrialist in my working methods."

Plate Glass Vase #28/08 (no.18), is an example of the original Vase series. The static geometric contour is playfully interrupted by a core spiral suggestive of a DNA structure. Three dyes—pink, orange, and yellow—added to the different adhesive stripes become visible depending on one's point of view.

In Hutter's Quasi Modern and RA Quasi Modern series (no.19), the objects are the negative image of the vase form. With the interplay of negative and positive spaces, created by stacking planes of glass, this series as well as the Solid Vase Form series tries to embody more volumetric images. Of his Cubic Heart Vase series, Hutter says, "the outer surface contours imply a pointillist view, while the interior shows a rectilinear structure reminiscent of a building under construction." In the most recent series, the vessel is dominated by vertically placed plate glass, in other words the original vase on its side.

Sidney Hutter has developed a strong vocabulary of form and technique that will enable him to continue redefining his original vase concept. Recently, he has indicated that he may begin working in hot, as well as cold, glass.

RVG

Sidney R. Hutter
Plate Glass Vase #28/08, no. 18
Museum of Fine Arts, Boston

Kreg Kallenberger

As Chloe Zerwick observed in her *Short History of Glass,* glass has served for centuries as "a symbol of clarity, spiritual perfection, and revelation [and] as a metaphor for a level of existence between the visible and the invisible, or between the mundane and the mysterious." Kreg Kallenberger's works, made of optical-quality lead crystal, exemplify these attributes of glass, as they draw the viewer into their interiors, revealing an illusionary world that embraces both the sublime and the beautiful.

Kallenberger's work has proceeded in a progression of named series, such as Cuneiform, Interlock, Titanic, Reservoir, and Osage. Each series begins with a batch of cast glass blanks, which, after careful annealing, are taken to the cold shop. There they are cut, ground, sandblasted, polished, stained, and otherwise manipulated, as each blank gradually reveals its hidden potential. The resultant images on the rough, irregular base of the object are enhanced and amplified by the prismatic and refractive properties of the cast-glass forms; the image changes with the viewer's perspective.

View at Saddleback Ridge (no. 20) is part of the Osage series, named for the hills near the artist's studio outside Tulsa, Oklahoma. It is, at first glance, a substantial wedge of glass with highly polished, reflective sides. A yellowish ellipse at the center of the top and a triangular pointer are the first clues that something extraordinary may be happening inside. Upon approach, the viewer is startled by the seemingly magical appearance of a rugged interior landscape featuring jagged mountains and running streams in brown, green, and blue. The surface of the glass has been heavily sandblasted, and alkyd oils were applied wet and

then wiped away immediately, leaving the resultant stain. Kallenberger links this work to paintings by Albert Bierstadt, artists of the Hudson River School, and other nineteenth-century American painters, but notes that his Osage series landscapes, although also indebted to the Oklahoma countryside, are ultimately imaginary, rather than realistic, depictions of specific places. They convey a sense of monumentality that belies their size.

Kallenberger's family moved to Tulsa when he was an infant, and he has remained there ever since. He received both his bachelor's and master's degrees from the University of Tulsa, where he studied mechanical engineering before switching to art. He became interested in glass in 1972 while working on his master's degree in ceramics. After graduation, he established the school's first glass studio, where he taught for several years. His work has received increasing critical attention in the last fifteen years, allowing him to become an independent artist, and it is now included in more than twenty-five public collections.

GWRW

Kreg Kallenberger
View at Saddleback Ridge, 1990 (no. 20)
Museum of Fine Arts, Boston

Joey Kirkpatrick and Flora C. Mace

"Our differences make it work . . . if we were the same, we'd be redundant," Joey Kirkpatrick says of her collaboration with Flora C. Mace, which began during Kirkpatrick's first Pilchuck summer in 1979.

Kirkpatrick came to glass through drawing, painting, and printmaking, which she continues to work on independently. In the late 1970s she produced a series of figurative watercolors, which she and Mace wanted to incorporate into glass vessels. Mace had helped Dale Chihuly (q.v.) "draw" the evocative images in his Blanket series (no. 6; later Kirkpatrick also worked on the Blanket series). However, the figures presented new difficulties. Mace is the problem solver of the duo; she thinks three-dimensionally with ease and is a natural builder of things—currently Mace builds boats. Mace's development of a figural technique epitomizes the innovative spirit of the early glass movement when artists, with a minimum of technical knowledge, were searching for ways in which to express their ideas in glass. Solutions were inventive and supplies came from unpredictable sources. For *The Conversation* (no. 22), Mace bought an ordinary hotplate at a hardware store on which to heat a steel plate. The plate provided the hot surface on which to lay out the figures that had been shaped with hand-bent wire and to melt colored glass within the wire forms. The fragile, colored drawings were applied to partially blown glass cylinders and laboriously worked into the surface. Because wire would expand and be pulled out of shape with additional blowing, it was snipped at critical junctures. Additional color details were added with a torch and glass threads. Lively gestural figures—not without an aura of solemn thoughtfulness—are the result of Kirkpatrick's and Mace's hybrid expression.

The idea of collaborating on glass fruits was conceived in 1988, on one of their many sojourns back to Pilchuck. Buoyed by the bucolic setting, Kirkpatrick and Mace wanted to produce something totally different during their two-week tenure. The idea of incorporating life-sized glass fruit in a wooden sculpture evolved and together they managed to fashion an apple, a pear, and a peach. Kirkpatrick and Mace had particular roles in producing the fruit—Mace blew the glass fruits and stems, together they shaped the fruits, and Kirkpatrick dusted on particles of colored glass that suggest the touch of her watercolors. While Kirkpatrick and Mace maintain aesthetic control, they also depend upon a team of assistants.

The colossal *Still Life* (no. 23) is the largest of their glass sculptures produced thus far. While enlarging fruit to this size increases the work's objectness—that is, the viewer is confronted with large shapes of joyous color—age-old fruit symbolism cannot be avoided. Fruit represents fullness, fecundity, and life, and to magnify fruits to this extent is to glory in all that they convey. This adulation is a kind of idolizing, an apotheosis of fruits. To present the fruits on a platter extends the notion of enthronement or enshrinement, a metaphor for life held sacred.

LFN

Joey Kirkpatrick and Flora C. Mace
Still Life, 1997 (no. 23)
Collection of the artists

Jon Kuhn

After receiving his B.F.A. from Washburn University in Topeka, Kansas, in 1972, Jon Kuhn moved to Richmond, Virginia, working first as a potter in his own studio and then as a mill worker. His affinity for woodworking led Kuhn to study furniture making at Virginia Commonwealth University.

At Virginia Commonwealth, Kuhn turned from furniture making to glass blowing, receiving his M.F.A. in 1978. An example of his early work, *CTVS #44* (no. 24), exhibits the seeds of his current process. *CTVS #44* is blown, with a section cut away and polished to reveal a multicolored interior pattern. The exterior is acid treated to give the surface a rough, eroded, and earthy finish, reminiscent of geological strata. At first glance the connection between the organic forms and surfaces of Kuhn's early blown work and the cool, mathematic perfection of his current, laminated work is somewhat obscure. But the continuity lies in the interior world of his intricate compositions.

A longtime devotee of Eastern philosophy, Kuhn meditates daily and believes that universal truths may be discovered through introspection. His aesthetic has always centered on a penetration of the exterior to reveal the brilliance within. By 1988 Kuhn had outfitted his Winston-Salem, North Carolina, studio with industrial technology, using optical sheet glass and industrial grinders. His sculptures are assembled around a core cube, composed of pieces of thinly ground and polished clear glass layered with colored powders and gold and silver leaf. The resulting stacks are fused and cut through; these striped cross sections are then laminated together to form a checkerboard block. Finally, this block is sliced, and the pieces then polished and lami-

nated so that colored and colorless pieces alternate at various intervals. Kuhn employs numerous assistants to aid him with the time-consuming grinding, cutting, and polishing. The core of *Desert Blush* is made of highly reflective and refractive lead fluoride glass that shatters the light passing through into its prismatic essence. The core is encased within nonreflective, nonrefractive, highly polished borasilicate plate glass, which allows the eye to easily penetrate the surface to concentrate on the explosive play of light and color within. The top and bottom sections of the column act as a foil to the fixed and perfect immobility of the core, incorporating the liquid energy of colored glass powder melted with sheet glass to produce a flowing stream of color.

The artist attributes his emphasis on intricate pattern to an interest in weaving, mathematics, and music. To the viewer, the meticulous constructions may also suggest a fantastical futuristic vision of cities in space. Kuhn delights in the clear and refractive nature of his medium; he has described his forms, and the light emanating from them, as "the architecture of a better world."

BMM

Jon Kuhn
Desert Blush, 1992 (no. 26)
Collection of the artist

Marvin Lipofsky

Marvin Lipofsky is a senior figure in the American studio glass movement. In 1964 he was among the first of Harvey K. Littleton's (q.v.) graduate students at the University of Wisconsin when hot glassworking moved from the factory into the artist's studio. The same year, Lipofsky introduced glass as an art form into the curriculum of the department of design at the University of California, Berkeley. There he continued to teach until 1972. He also

headed the glass department as a full professor at the California College of Arts and Crafts from 1967 to 1987. Lipofsky has traveled extensively in Holland, Italy, the Czech Republic, Sweden, Finland, Japan, and China, collaborating with master glassblowers in their own studios and in factories. Master glassmaker Stefan Stefko and his team from Czechoslovakia contributed to the vessel illustrated here (no. 29).

Lipofsky holds M.S. and M.F.A. degrees from the University of Wisconsin, both in sculpture, so it is not surprising that his works are strongly form-oriented. He makes his tools and molds as extensions of his hands in order to sculpt his glass. The organic freedom of his work recalls the freedom with which abstract expressionist painters attacked their canvasses throughout the 1950s and 1960s. But the variety of transparency and opacity of glass offers a chance to explore elements not available to painters. Lipovsky also explores the interior spaces of his sculpture by sawing them open or sawing openings into the forms. Exteriors are frosted with sandblasting while interiors are left glossy. The

results are sensual. A viewer may relate almost any visual reference imagined to works by Lipofsky, for they are as unparticularized as they are universal in their imagery.

Lipofsky's sculpture creates the impression of semi-transparent tissues, bladders, organs, flesh, and mammiform shapes, flowers, shells, and other shapes with female associations. His titles carry such atmospheric images as *Morning Mist, Summer Rain,* and *Pacific Sunset.*

"It's an exciting material," says Lipofsky. "It fights you physically . . . you know you've got your skill, you know you're pretty good, but then you also know that something can go wrong." It is this quality of risk in workmanship that separates art from manufactured goods. Liposky deftly captures the breathtaking moment when one process must stop and another begins—when the glass becomes frozen in time. After cooling, Lipofsky's work undergoes further alteration by cutting, hand grinding, and sandblasting. At every step risks are taken to enhance the work and bring it closer to perfection.

Lipofsky's residence and studio remain in Berkeley, California. More than thirty major public museums hold his work in permanent collections. His exhibition and award record is extensive. As a university professor and a teacher at many workshops and craft schools, his influence upon the world of contemporary glass is immeasurable.

JLF

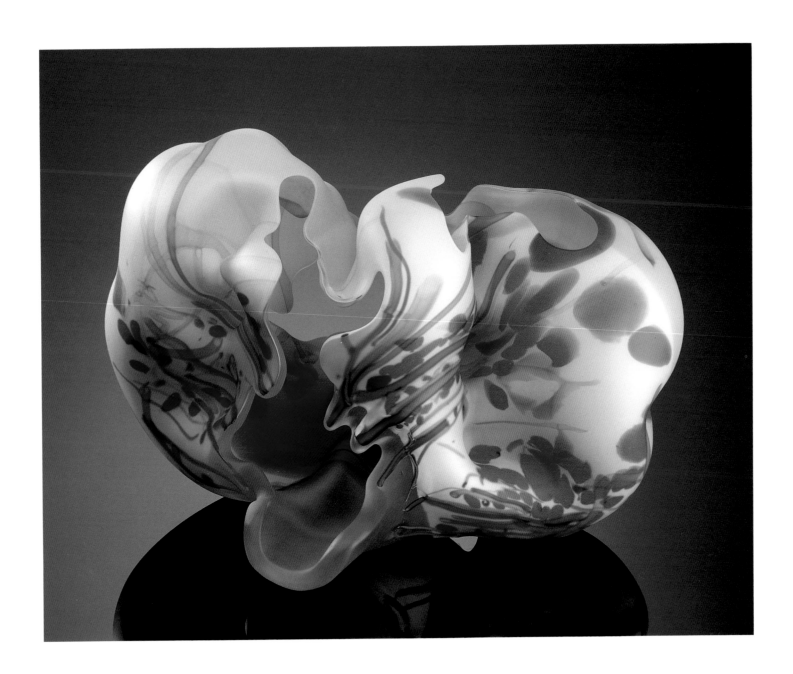

Marvin Lipofsky, with Stefan Stefko and team
IGS III Series 1988-93 #4, 1988-93 (no. 29)
Collection of the artist

Andrew Magdanz

Andrew Magdanz ascribes his initial involvement with the studio glass movement to the Kent State murders of 1970. At the time, Magdanz was attending Dunwoody Industrial Institute in Minneapolis along with many Vietnam veterans who were there on the GI bill. When news of the killings was announced over the school's public address system,

a loud cheer went up for the Ohio National Guardsmen. Later that day, Doug Johnson, his former junior high school art teacher and a ceramist and sculptor who had worked with Harvey K. Littleton (q.v.), encouraged Magdanz to study at the University of Wisconsin, known for its anti-war atmosphere. After receiving his industrial certificate in mold-making and machinery tool-and-die making, Magdanz received a B.S. and M.A. from the University of Wisconsin, where he assisted Littleton. He completed his formal training under Marvin Lipofsky (q.v.) at the California College of Arts and Crafts, earning an M.F.A. in 1978.

Magdanz's work bears little resemblance to that of his mentors, whom he credits with providing a work ethic. Magdanz's work has evolved from simple forms that activated the surrounding space with projecting elements, to quieter pieces that produce a dialogue between interior and exterior surfaces. In the past two years, he has experimented with a new, broken surface, to which he has introduced color. Although Magdanz's work is structurally stable, his forms have an air of instability and a lightness that at times seems to defy gravity.

In addition to his solo work, Magdanz has participated in collaborative ventures for architectural lighting and public sculptures. He also operates a studio with partners for the production of such commercial craft items as pitchers, vases, bowls, and bottles. His production line frees Magdanz from putting financial constraints on his art pieces, but it also means he produces but ten to fifteen sculptures annually. In addition to starting the glass program at Colorado Mountain College, Magdanz often has taught during summers at the Pilchuck Glass School, the Haystack School, and the Penland School of Crafts.

The recipient of two National Endowment for the Arts grants, Magdanz was awarded in 1979 a Master Craftsman Grant. The masterwork he produced during his graduate program and finished during this fellowship was entitled *Return to the Safety of the Sanctum,* a reference to the glass community. Collected by numerous public and private institutions in the United States and abroad, including the Corning Museum of Glass and the Hokkaido Museum of Modern Art in Sapporo, Japan, Magdanz's work is represented in the Museum of Fine Arts collection with *Three Spirals* of 1988 (1992.279).

RAGR

Andrew Magdanz
Vessel, 1997 (no. 32)
Collection of the artist

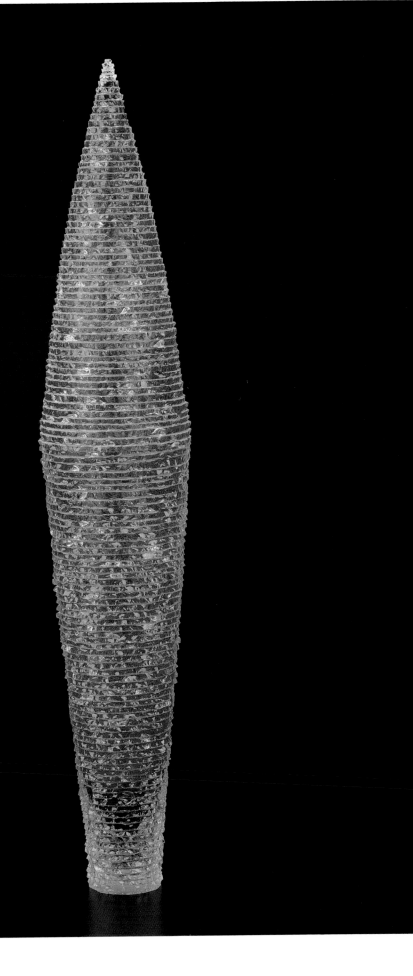

Dante Marioni

The objects in this exhibition are fashioned by people who can best be defined as artists; a few are uncomfortable with this term, but it expresses the way they are perceived by collectors and curators. Most of these individuals have received formal art training in colleges and universities, and most produce nonfunctional decorative objects that they refer

to as sculpture. Dante Marioni, the youngest person whose work is included in this show, is something of an exception to these generalizations. While he is certainly an artist, he has been trained more in the craftsman traditions of the workplace than in the academy, and he is most noted for his interpretations of classical Greek forms which are instantly recognizable as functional vessels (even if they are never to be so used).

He was born in Mill Valley, California, the son of the noted glassmaker Paul Marioni (b. 1941), who learned his craft from Marvin Lipofsky (q.v.). At the age of nine Dante received his first glassblowing experience in the shop of Jay Musler (q.v.). The Marionis moved to Seattle in 1979, and thus landed in the fertile center of the studio glass movement. During the next few years, Dante had the opportunity to apprentice and train with several masters in the Italian tradition, including Benjamin Moore in Seattle and Fritz Dreisbach at the Penland School in North Carolina. He met and learned from older American glassmakers, including Dale Chihuly (q.v.) and Richard Marquis (see a so-called *Shard Whopper* vase by Marioni and Marquis [no. 41]). He had the extraordinary opportunity to train with Lino

Tagliapietra while the Italian master was teaching at the Pilchuck Glass School. In 1985 Marioni traveled to Venice, investigating on his own the history and techniques of glassmaking.

Marioni opened his own workshop in Seattle in 1984, and by 1987 he had his own successful gallery show. Recognition came swiftly; among other honors, he received a Louis Comfort Tiffany fellowship in 1987 and was honored the next year by the American Craft Museum through their inclusion of his work in their "Young Americans" exhibition. Today his glass is in many collections in the United States and abroad, including the White House Collection of American Crafts. His work is exhibited widely, and he has taught extensively at Pilchuck and at workshops in many varied locations.

Superbly proportioned and large in scale, Marioni's vessels—modern versions of such classical ceramic forms as the kylix, amphora, and oinochoe—often lack surface decoration (no. 37). They are sleek, cool, strongly colored, elegant forms that speak to the long tradition of fine glassblowing. Marioni often uses one bright color for the body of his vessels, highlighting with black or another color such features as handles, knops, and midbands, echoing the way glaze was applied to his ancient prototypes. *Topaz Mosaic Vase* (no. 36) is produced using murrini canes that give its surface an overall mosaic appearance. The mosaic squares are placed on the marver side by side, fused together, then picked up and blown. Distortion during blowing gives the finished product its all-over, craquelure appearance.

GWRW

Dante Marioni
Topaz Mosaic Vase, 1995 (no. 36)
Collection of Andrea and Charles Bronfman

Richard Marquis

Richard Marquis's work has been variously described as outrageous, heretical, impudent, and whimsical. At the same time, it reveals a talent for creating the stylish and the beautiful.

In 1969 Marquis was awarded a Fulbright Scholarship to learn the murrine technique at the Venini Factory in Italy. He is the first contemporary American glass artist to use this process, familiar from glass paperweights filled with thousands of colorful stylized flowers (millefiori) and other silhouette shapes. Known to the Egyptians, murrini was perfected in sixteenth-century Venice and reinterpreted by Carlo Scarpa for the Venini Factory during the 1940s. Different colored glass rods are fused together into bundles about three inches wide and six inches long. These rods are then reheated and pulled until pencil thin. To obtain a silhouette of a horse, a teapot, etc., molten glass is dipped into a one-piece mold, cooled, dipped into another color of glass, and then pulled as above. These rods or canes are sliced and fused to make the desired piece.

Marquis is known primarily for his teapots (nos. 37 and 39) and for his Marquiscarpa pieces (no. 38). These latter pieces, which are derived from ancient chalices, from African and Asian headrests, and from glassware designed by Carlo Scarpa, often feature unexpected and colorful silhouettes mixed in with the solid colors of the tray or stem. In other pieces, such as *Venus de Marquis* (1985), slices of murrini cane are fused to the outside of a blown glass shape.

Cup with Toothbrush Feet (no. 40) is composed of a blown banana-like shape with a blue cup on top, the yellow "body" resting on four toothbrushes, bristles serving as the feet. The checkered plastic handles of the toothbrushes

(purchased in Germany) are a prelude to his murrini Marquiscarpa pieces and are part of his Fabricated Weird series, begun in 1974, in which he mixes blown, cast, or lampworked glass with found objects. (Marquis's home, on an island in Puget Sound, is filled with rubber squeeze toys, Christmas lights, antique car models, and plastic salt and pepper shakers that he might need one day.)

Born in Bumblebee, Arizona, Marquis participated in the 1967 "Funk Art" exhibition at the University Art Museum, Berkeley, celebrating self-sufficiency and the handmade. He received his B.A. from the University of California at Berkeley in 1972. A pioneer at the Pilchuck School, he has taught in Seattle, and in the Bay Area of California, and has spent time in Tasmania, Australia. In addition to the Fulbright, he has received three grants from the National Endowment for the Arts, a Senior Fulbright Grant to New Zealand, and two grants from the Australian Crafts Council. He has been involved in two glass production businesses, one of which was called "Hippies Out To Make It Rich, etc." In 1987 Marquis went entirely on his own, enabling him to create whatever he wanted. His works are found in many museums in the United States and abroad.

ADM

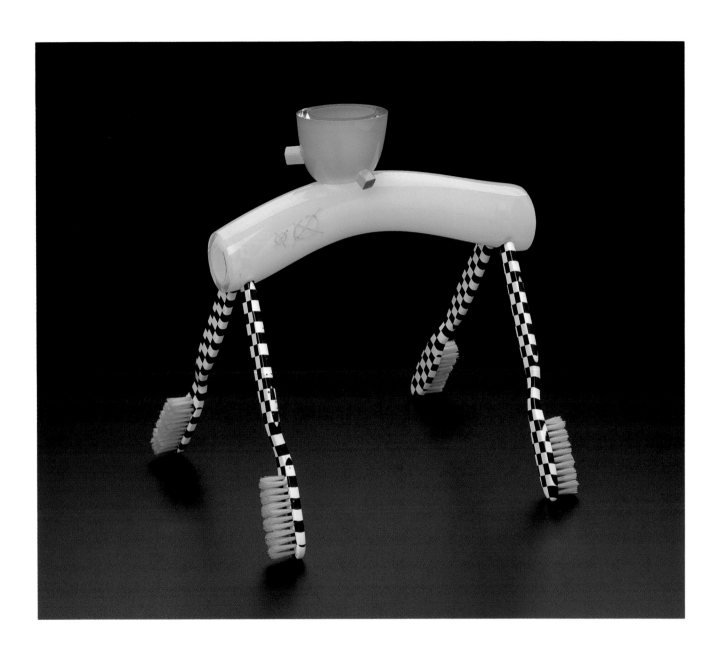

Richard Marquis
Cup with Toothbrush Feet, 1980 (no. 40)
Collection of Susan Shapiro Magdanz

William Morris

William Morris is one of the most distinctive studio glass artists at work today. His blown glass objects of the 1980s and 1990s evoke the early history of man and the earth, with references, for example, to the cave paintings of prehistoric France and Spain and the funerary arts of ancient Egyptians. These mysterious pieces have been developed in series, ranging from the relatively simple, natural forms in the Standing Stone, Stone Vessel, River Rock, and Burial Urn series, to more complex, anthropological constructs in series entitled Suspended Artifact, Canopic Jar, and Rhyton. Evoking both natural objects and man-made artifacts that might have been unearthed archaeologically, these recent works stimulate contemplation of the elements of continuity and discontinuity in man's long history.

Antelope (no. 43) and *Big Horn Sheep* (no. 42) represent a revival of the Egyptian canopic jar, used in sets of four as part of the mummification process for the preservation of the deceased's liver, lungs, stomach, and intestines. While Egyptian jars have heads fashioned in the form of the baboon, falcon, jackal, and man, each a son of the god Horus, the appropriate deity, Morris has substituted heads derived from wildlife, and in place of the Egyptian hieroglyphic inscriptions, he uses images more akin to cave paintings. The Morris canopic jars appear almost to be ceramic objects. He applies powdered glass to them at several stages to give them an antique look, testimony to Morris's desire to eliminate the "glassiness" of his art. His current Rhyton series, named for ancient drinking vessels with the base in the shape of an animal's or woman's head, carries this sculptural look even farther.

Morris blows his glass in the traditional manner and builds it, sculpturing forms from solid molten glass. He works in a

shop setting, assisted by what used to be called journeymen and apprentices, each of whom has worked with him for periods ranging from five to twenty years. His assistants have included Randy Walker, Karen Willinbrink, and Jon Ormbrek. Using a technique related to Navajo sand painting, Ormbrek, among other tasks, has been responsible for the Cro-Magnon era figures in powdered glass that have often embellished Morris's designs. Ormbrek's hand is represented in this exhibition in *Suspended Artifact* (no. 44), with its depictions of long-horned animals. This assemblage and others of its kind appear to have been created by a shaman for some sort of ritual whose exact meaning has been lost.

Morris grew up in Carmel, California, where he enjoyed rock climbing and exploring for artifacts in the surrounding hills, youthful experiences that have contributed to the look of his adult work. He attended California State University and Central Washington University with largely indifferent results. The watershed in his life occurred when he obtained a position as a summer truck driver at the Pilchuck Glass School in 1978. He quickly became a protegé and chief assistant to Dale Chihuly (q.v.), and his relationship with Pilchuck continues to the present. Morris's first major individual exhibition came in 1980, and he has compiled a distinguished professional record since then.

GWRW

William Morris
Canopic Jar: Big Horn Sheep, 1995 (no. 42)
Collection of Dale and Doug Anderson

Jay Musler

"My compulsiveness," says Jay Musler, "is not in the techniques of my work but in the method of reflecting my thoughts." His reflections range from "air and laughter" and "light and freedom" to "confusion" and "mental torment." Ben Marks states that Musler's approach has been to dig as deep a conceptual hole as he can and then try to get himself out of it.

A native of Sacramento, California, Musler was drawn to art through the influence of his high school art teacher.

He participated in the pilot program of the California College of Arts and Crafts in Oakland, where he came under the influence of Marvin Lipovsky (q.v.). Work in a production glass studio for the next ten years enabled him to become an expert foot and stem maker and mold blower, as shown in *Five Goblets* (no. 46). Here, although the viewer is prevented from reaching the contents of the goblet's bowl by thorns, wire, and other impedimenta on the stems, the delectable colors and flower-like shapes beckon and speak of future delights.

Musler began his artistic career with the creation of bowls of sandblasted and painted forms cut from moldblown glass balls. Sometimes he used blank Pyrex. This common and useful form is associated with pleasures—food, drink, flowers. However, about 1978 Musler began destroying the bowl form by introducing jagged, cruel edges, barbed wire, and pierced interiors, thus jarring his viewers with these hints of the horrors of war (see no. 48). Inspired by boats abandoned in a canal outside his studio in San Francisco, he next turned to that shape, first working from a bell jar and later from sandblasted and cut glass sticks that he made himself. Musler's boats were skeletal wrecks, not glorious galleons, yet at the same time a positive message may be read from them as transportation and travel are often stimulating and happy pursuits. The third phase came with the creation of masks that he first made from half of a glass cone, sometimes with an eye or other details painted on, which he mounted on bases made from glass sticks (see no. 47). Later he constructed the entire mask from these sticks. Like the boat series, the masks carry a double message, that of menacing and unknown deception and, on the other hand, of frivolity and mirth.

Jay Musler is an artist who truly makes the viewer think. He opens one's mind to a gamut of emotions and to a host of interpretations—from a "time for mourning" to a "time for dancing" (Ecclesiastes 3:1-11). He works from the inside out, from the private to the public, from a hidden message to a resounding proclamation. This is what enables him to climb out of those deep holes.

Jay Musler's work is in the collections of many museums in this country as well as in the Hokkaido Museum of Modern Art, Sapporo, Japan. He has received fellowships from the California Arts Council and the National Endowment for the Arts.

ADM

Jay Musler
Mask House, 1987 (no. 47)
Collection of Dale and Doug Anderson

Joel Philip Myers

The Contiguous Fragment series, to which *Arctic Summer* (no. 49), *Ørding Garden I* (no. 50), and *Valmuen* (Red Poppies) V (no. 51) belong, discloses Joel Philip Myers's romantic and formal concerns. Myers, who gardens earnestly at his Danish home, finds inspiration in his garden and surrounding landscape, transforming fields of flowers into a sea of colored glass. Myers's work grapples with the formal concerns of his artistic generation, conveying a visual structure that may be likened to the large-scale stain paint-

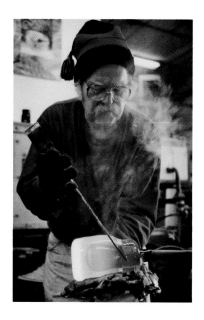

ings of, for example, Helen Frankenthaler. Myers's heavily walled vessels possess an actuality and a weight that conveys the sense of space being filled and acted upon. As spherical forms are blown they are flattened into ovoids because Myers was, by his own confession, "greedy" for a larger canvas, which appears even larger by Myers's carefully scaled elements. Glass as pure color nearly overtakes the volume; colors emanate from inside, meld into the surface, inch around the thin volume, and radiate through the vessel wall behind.

Myers's work conveys a glory in its sensuality, which at the same time implies nature's—or love's—fragile, passing reality. Technically, Myers has pushed glass to the utmost and developed a process sympathetic to his expressive concerns. Blowing a vessel the size of *Ørding Garden I* (no. 50) is a physical and technical feat. At several stages of gathering and blowing, eggshell-thin shards of colored glass that Myers has blown beforehand are incorporated into the vessel. The shards, arranged on a tray like paints on a palette, are held in an annealing furnace. Pulling colored shards from the tray with tweezers, Myers builds compositions on a graphite cloth laid on the cold steel marver to keep the glass

at the proper temperature and to impart the vessel's surface texture. The colored shards are then picked up by the blown form. Myers's vessels contain successive layers of shard combinations—some enclosed by additional gathers and some merging with the outer surface.

During Myers's graduate years in the College of Ceramics at Alfred University (1960-63), the head designer from Blenko Glass, a West Virginia factory that produces handcrafted glassware, arrived on campus to lecture. Myers was smitten by the art of glassmaking. Although Myers could not attend the Toledo Glass Workshops organized by Harvey K. Littleton (q.v.), he was impressed with what Littleton was attempting to do. Upon graduation, Myers was offered the post of head designer at Blenko. The Blenko workshop offered Myers the unique opportunity to be both designer and glassblower, allowing him creative freedom and encouraging his experimentation. By 1966 Myers had won the Best of Show in an exhibition at the Mint Museum of Art, Charlotte, North Carolina, and an Award of Merit from the Museum of Contemporary Crafts, New York. In 1970 Myers joined the faculty of Illinois State University to start a program through which he was to influence several second-generation glassmakers. Myers retired from his position as Distinguished Professor of Art in the spring of 1997. Numerous achievements and honors underline Joel Philip Myers's seminal contribution to the studio glass movement.

LFN

Joel Philip Myers
Ørding Garden I, 1988 (no. 50)
Collection of Daniel Greenberg and Susan Steinhauser

Thomas Patti

Tom Patti developed his unique approach to glassworking in relative isolation from the mainstream of the hot-glass studio movement of the 1960s and 1970s. After briefly encountering glassblowing at the Penland School in 1970, Patti returned to Massachusetts and began experimenting with salvaged Vitrolite and sheet glass, using a self-built furnace and idiosyncratic equipment he built from scratch. Six years later he had produced a body of work unique in the glass world. His first solo exhibition was organized by art dealer Douglas Heller in New York City.

Patti's glass is made up of hovering layers of fused plates worked in sequences of progressive forms shaped under pressures from within. Relationships between the planes of glass invite the viewer to explore voids and passages, changing colors, structural repetitions, refraction, and other optical gestures produced through and shaped by fire or heat. Just as rhythmic units on plants and animals are structured according to use, so also is Patti's glass structured through strata and modular units. Pressing through strata, a bubble or spherical shape rises to unify and magically affect the rectilinear solid mass. Balance between mechanistically perfect layers and fluid shaping of voids reminds the viewer of the medium's dual nature, both solid and liquid.

The five-part *Division of Fifty, Luminated Particles for Doug* (no. 52) consists of fused, hand-formed, ground, and polished glass spheroids that captivate the imagination by their exterior simplicity and interior complexity. Within each sphere is an intriguing swirl of layers that are integral to the form—one cannot exist without the other. The spheroids suggest the beauty of extraordinary gemstones or large natural crystals formed through pressure and heat from deep within the earth or from cosmic space. That reference offers a clue to comprehending the majestic but enigmatic work of Tom Patti. No evidence of the artist's hand is referenced in his works; it is as if the artist were a silent, or extremely quiet, partner of thought rather than a workman. Patti's art is not one of bravura—it is usually small in scale—but conceptually his work is monumental. He has produced public sculpture on a grand scale, but he is best known for art that can be held quietly in the hand for contemplation.

Patti is an honors graduate (1969) of Pratt Institute, Brooklyn, New York, and holds a master's degree in industrial design. He has received many grants, awards, fellowships, and honors. His works are to be seen in more than twenty major museums both in the United States and abroad. Since the mid-1970s he has maintained an active exhibition record from his studio in Plainfield, Massachusetts. For this exhibition Patti created a new work displayed at the entrance, *Spectral Gateway* (no. 54).

JLF

Thomas Patti

Division of Fifty, Luminated Particles for Doug, 1993 (no. 52)

Collection of Dale and Doug Anderson

Ginny Ruffner

Two words leap to mind when one thinks of Ginny Ruffner--humor and imagination. Although Ruffner works in lampwork, the technique used to make the famous glass flowers at Harvard's Botanical Museum, from here on all resemblance ends. Ruffner uses many floral forms, as well as those of various mammals, but in her work they are stylized, fantasized, and colorful well beyond the bounds of nature.

Ruffner received her B.A. (1974) and her M.F.A. (1975) from the University of Georgia where she majored in drawing and painting. Her ambition was not always to be an artist; in fact, she has said that she didn't know who Michelangelo was until she was in college. Her interest in glass began when she saw a Marcel Duchamp painting on two glass panes. She apprenticed as an engraver in a glass shop in Atlanta and after a year moved up to apprentice lampworker. In this process a glass rod is heated over a flame and delicately shaped with tools. Ruffner takes this method several steps further in creating a pitted surface by sandblasting the annealed glass. This surface will hold paint and even pastels. Her first pieces, however, were conventional goblets of clear glass. An inkling of what lay ahead was apparent in the stems of some, fashioned as dragonflies, crocodiles, or vegetables.

In 1985 Ruffner moved to Seattle where she began to teach nontraditional lampworking. Her first sculpture showing imagery—shoes—was made in 1986. During the next three years she began creating story lines and titles. The latter she sees as "turning off points," providing the viewer a little information enabling interpretation in his or her own way. She began to shade the glass with paint and to incorporate miniatures of works by Picasso, Monet, Botticelli, and oth-

ers into her sculptures. She created still lifes—*Still Glass* and *Beauty Surfing through a Still Life* (both 1989)—and public art, including the entry portal for the South Park Community Center in Seattle (1989). From 1989 through 1991 she created nearly one hundred lampwork pieces.

Ruffner has always believed that the one constant in life is change. In December 1991 change came to her in the form of a traffic accident that left her paralyzed, speechless, and without memory. She remained in a coma for five weeks.

"You don't realize how much the brain does," Ruffner says, "until it doesn't." Grueling therapy brought her back to work. She has not lost her "intellectual playfulness." *It's All In How You View It* is the title of a sculpture of a wheelchair decorated with streamers and propelled by blue birds of happiness. Prior to her accident, Ruffner's work was turbulent, contorted, and offered facets for interpretation. Post-accident it seems gentler, more introspective, and, unbelievably, more humorous: the glass fish in the rhinestone spectacles, the cowboy boots with red hearts, the chicken's mischievous eye, the "balance" figures in striped jerseys, the miniature Picasso. *What Is a Style?* (no. 57) is a framework of blown glass balls carrying various symbols, such as the suits on playing cards, enclosing a crazy quilt of color and design. It poses its title question, but surely does not answer it.

ADM

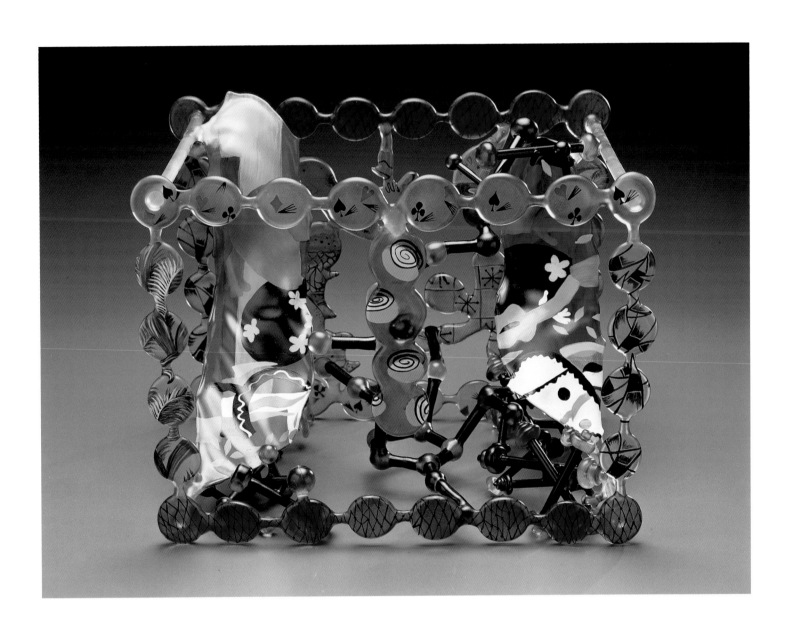

Ginny Ruffner
What Is a Style?, 1997 (no. 57)
Collection of the artist

Mary Shaffer

Mary Shaffer was trained as a painter, earning a B.F.A. in painting and illustration from the Rhode Island School of Design in 1965 and a M.F.A. in painting from the University of Maryland in 1987. Fascinated with windows and light, but frustrated by her attempts to capture them on canvas, she turned to glass. Since the early seventies her work has defined slumping. This is a process previously developed by the furniture and auto industries, in which glass is heated until it bends to conform to a shape determined by a containing mold.

Temperature and time of heating are very important aspects of this process.

The artist calls her principal technique "mid-air slumping." This process involves firing fine plate glass in a kiln. Once the temperature curve is set and the situation is structured, the slumping proceeds almost without intervention. The artist's passivity to her material results from her deep belief, related to Buddhism, that "in order for humanity to survive, we have to work with nature following the female principle of bending and following with nature, not imposing one's will on it."

The central theme in Shaffer's work, the unquiet harmony of opposites, can be recognized in *Wall Treasures II* (no. 60), showing several miniature tools in combination with glass. *Tool Wall* (no. 59) was later developed from this earlier piece. Both *Tool Wall* and *Wall Treasures II* deal with the fluidity and clarity of the glass juxtaposed with the idiosyncratic character of the discarded tools; in *Red Hook* (no. 58), a bright element of color provides a contrasting, ambiguous feeling. Some of the tools are dipped in hot glass, on others the glass is cast or slumped. By using old tools as representative of the obsolete artifacts of our culture, Shaffer wants to show respect for the craftsmanship inherent in the tools and to restore their symbolic value.

In Shaffer's Inversion series a finished glass piece is used to make a mold; then the mold is cast in bronze. The two pieces are then displayed side by side as a pair. Shaffer's ability to create a sense of movement frozen in time exploits the fragility of glass, while simultaneously demonstrating its strength.

For her larger commissioned work, which can reach up to sixty feet in height, Shaffer also uses metal in combination with stone. The stone in a way replaces the glass, for the underlying concept stays the same. The intention behind all her work is "to take you out of yourself through visual stimulation to a different plane of understanding."

RVG

Mary Shaffer
Wall Treasures II, 1993 (no. 60)
Collection of Simona and Jerome Chazen

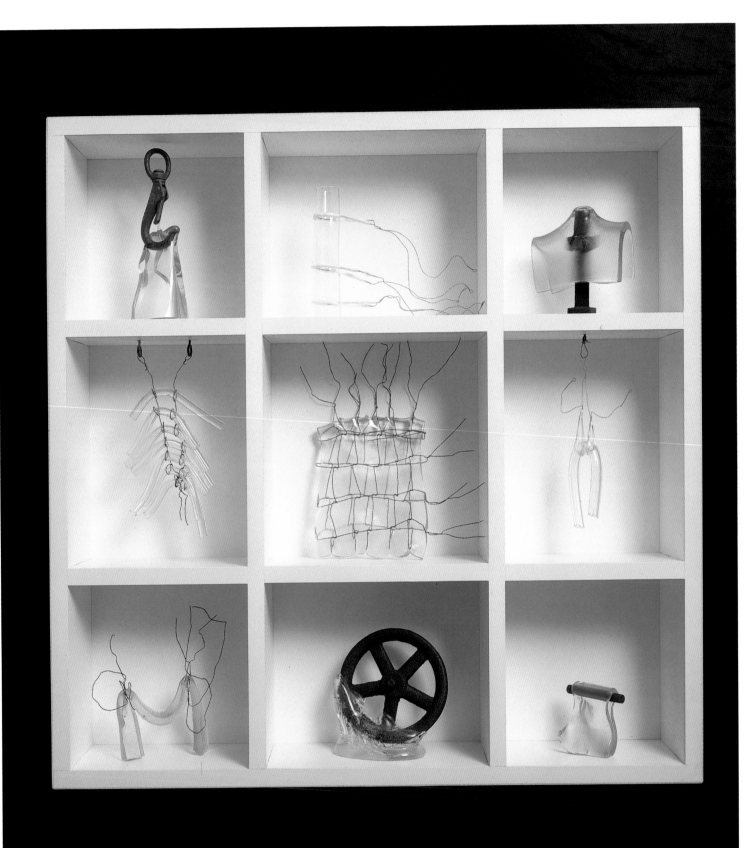

Paul J. Stankard

One of America's best-known paperweight makers, Paul Stankard graduated in 1963 from Salem County Vocational Technical Institute, New Jersey, where he received a diploma in glassblowing technology. After working in the scientific glass industry for ten years, Stankard became a full-time paperweight maker in 1972. His high level of technical skill  at flameworking in combination with his chosen glass form, the paperweight, makes his work distinctive in the contemporary glass movement. Stankard's emphasis on precision and accuracy contrasts with the focus on coincidence and improvisation taught at Pilchuck Glass School.

Nature and wildflowers in particular have inspired Stankard from the beginning. People looking at Stankard's work for the first time wonder if he has encapsulated the real flower in crystal glass, indicating the perfection of Stankard's technique. For several years the artist has also used the flameworking skills of some of his children at his studio, next to his home in Mantua, New Jersey. The plants and insects are made with colored glass and encapsulated in two globs of clear glass. This process, closely related to the paperweight technique and dating back to 1843, had been kept a secret for a long time. Stankard does not believe in keeping it a secret and therefore teaches the technique at several schools, including Pilchuck.

Stankard has advanced the paperweight concept by developing his columnar shaped "botanicals," which can be viewed not only from above, but from all directions. This new and larger form enabled Stankard to show the whole wildflower, including its roots. Furthermore, the botanicals no longer have a utilitarian function, holding down papers, but have become more of an art object.

A variation on the botanicals are the "cloistered" botanicals (no. 63), fairly large objects with laminated plates of dark blue or green glass to the back and sometimes the sides as well. These cloistered botanicals force the viewer back into a one-sided view, giving the impression of looking into a niche. Other forms that evolved from the botanicals are the diptych and triptych botanicals.

The Golden Bowl Diptych (no. 62) provides an excellent view of Stankard's netherworld with its root people. The arrangement of pink daisies, white alium, yellow coronet blossoms, and pale blue forget-me-nots is no longer the center of attention as the flowers were in Stankard's earlier paperweights. The root people, as Stankard calls them, have become more and more important in his work. These earth spirits should remind the viewer of mankind's inseparable connection with all life on earth, and all life's inseparable connection to God.

RVG

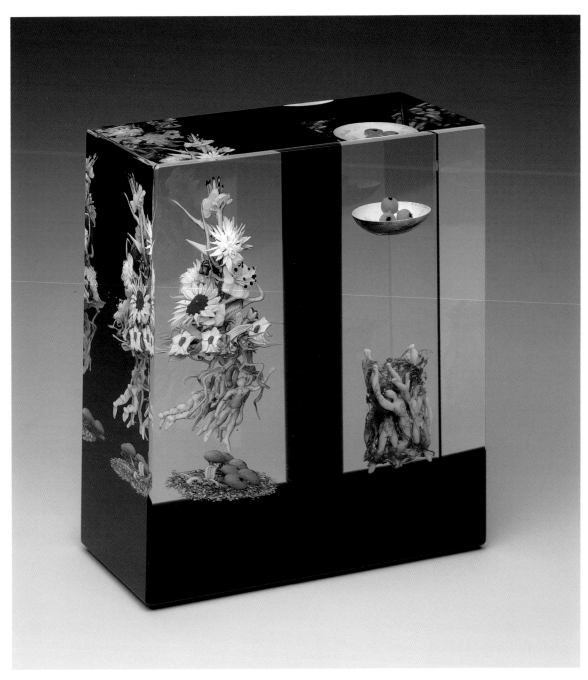

Paul J. Stankard
Golden Bowl Diptych, 1996 (no. 62)
Collection of Lois Sandler

Catherine ("Cappy") Thompson

The hard black outlines of *Fiddler* (no. 66) hark back to the lead cames in medieval stained glass that have always inspired Cappy Thompson. The undulating shape of the round glass vessel emphasizes the roundness of the figure and the sense of movement.

Thompson is not herself a glassblower. When she first began to paint on vessels she was given blanks by her fellow artists. As her reputation grew, she was able to design vessels which she then commissioned from such artists as Ben Moore and Dante Marioni (q.v.). The first firing of the piece takes place after the figural design is outlined on the outside with heavy black marker. The piece is laid horizontally on a light table and a gray wash is applied over the entire interior surface of the drawing (grisaille technique). The piece is fired a second time and highlights removed with dry brushes, thus giving texture and volume to the drawing. Transparent colors (enamels made from metal oxides) are applied to the interior of the piece, following a watercolor rendering made by the artist. The handles on Thompson's brushes have been cut short to enable her to manipulate them inside the vessel. The colors change when firing takes place. Increasingly we see the artist using more bright and jewel-like tones. She often layers colors and usually fires the vessel twice more to obtain the desired shades. Basically, Thompson's technique is that of *eglomisé* or reverse painting on glass which has been in existence for some two thousand years. Her vessels range in height from one to two feet, and in diameter up to fifteen inches. They are not intended for use: direct contact with water will, in time, erode the enamel.

Thompson was born in Alexandria, Virginia. She is now established outside Seattle, having arrived there via Evergreen State College in Olympia, Washington, where she received a B.A. in painting and printmaking. Artistically and technically self taught, her first job was in a small stained glass studio. After making her first piece in 1975, she soon found the vessel shape better suited to her narrative designs. She could depict two chapters or scenes, one on the front and one on the back *(Adoration of the Cosmic Cow,* 1995); represent two or three different characters (*Three Queens,* commissioned by J.C. Penney for Beverly Sills, 1996); or even add a third dimension to the front of the picture by using the back wall (*My Life with Lord Krishna,* 1994).

For Thompson, the narrative is paramount, whether she is depicting fairy tales, myths, picture poems, or stories incorporating aspects of her own life. Sometimes her figures and colors are influenced by Persian miniatures and Indian paintings. She depicts herself as a figure with silver hair, often with bangs, accompanied sometimes by her dog, sometimes by her husband, sometimes by make-believe animals. In *Searching for the Bodhisattva* (no. 65), Thompson appears as a haloed Madonna-like figure holding a telescope, seated in a canoe.

ADM

Catherine ("Cappy") Thompson
Fiddler, 1991 (no. 66)
Collection of Simona and Jerome Chazen

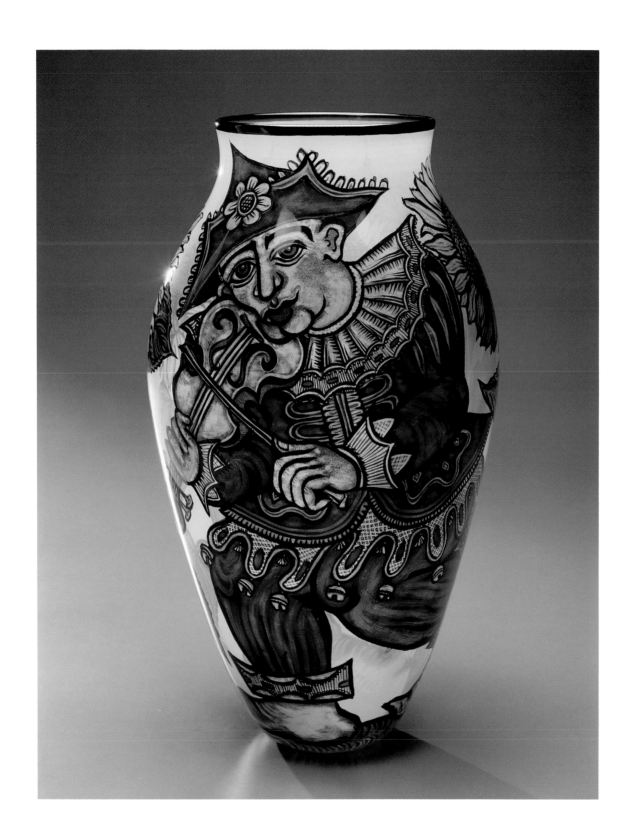

Karla Trinkley

Karla Trinkley's strong color sense grows out of her early training as a painter at the Tyler School of Art in Elkins Park, Pennsylvania, where she received her B.F.A. in 1979. She attributes her propensity for architectural exoskeletons to her exposure to oriental structures in an art history survey course and to oil holding tanks around the port of Philadelphia. As an undergraduate, Trinkley experimented with blowing pagoda shapes, but she did not find the process satisfactory. After reading an article by Minnie Rosenblatt on *pâte de verre,* literally "glass paste," she went to Rosenblatt's New York City gallery to view works created by this ancient Egyptian glass-casting technique. The unglass-like, sugary or waxy texture produced by this method appealed to Trinkley, and she determined to learn the technique.

In 1979, when Trinkley told Dale Chihuly (q.v.), her graduate school advisor at Rhode Island School of Design, that she wanted to perfect the *pâte de verre* casting technique in order to create interior forms encased within open exterior frameworks, Chihuly pronounced the goal unattainable. Until that time, due to technical limitations, *pâte de verre* work had been confined to small decorative motifs and naturalistic sculptures. Trinkley took Chihuly's discouragement as a challenge, and over the next two years, she engaged in countless experiments that resulted in a scientific method for producing cast glass.

The acknowledged master of this technique, Trinkley has found that by simplifying her process and maintaining strict control over temperatures in the kiln, she can almost guarantee a successful casting. Her husband, glass artist William Dexter, has engineered an oven with several independent heating zones. Often, Trinkley will leave enhancing mold fragments and residual clay deposited from the original model intact on the finished surface. The surface is usually matte, but may possess a wet translucency. Trinkley's works are distinguished further by a core of color and reflective light.

Trinkley's sculpture has been compared to art historical precedents, in particular to the diatretum or "cage cup," an ancient Roman vessel with an intricate outer weave of glass cut from a single piece of glass that exposes an inner vessel. The similarity is purely visual, however, as the artist was not referencing this form. Recently, Trinkley has emerged from a two-year sabbatical from glass. It will be interesting to observe how she develops the painted wooden forms she is introducing into her current work.

RAGR

Karla Trinkley
Terrapene, 1994 (no. 68)
Collection of the artist

Steven I. Weinberg

During the past fifteen years Steven Weinberg has transformed himself from formalist to poet. He received his B.F.A. from the New York State College of Ceramics at Alfred University. There his mentor in glass, Eric Hilton—a top designer at Steuben Glass—helped him "get over the fear of using beauty in a beautiful material." William Carlson, a glass artist who taught at the University of Illinois, Champaign, is Weinberg's "formal hero." Weinberg went on to earn his M.F.A. at the Rhode Island School of Design.

In his early work, Weinberg exerted a cool, compressed elegance into his tightly defined crystal spaces. Dynamic reflective surfaces act upon cast forms and the geometry is multiplied as the observer is drawn into the crystal world. The techniques Weinberg employed to achieve these pieces have remained essentially constant. Box molds encase plaster models that give negative form to the bottom field. Slabs of optical crystal are laid into the mold; as the glass responds to intense kiln heat, it slumps into the mold. Weinberg's captured bubble marks much of his early work. The bubble is air that rises during the heating process. If cooling does not begin at just the right moment, the bubble slips out of the top surface of molten glass. Following the cooling of the glass, outer geometric facets are polished to grab and reflect light; the under surface is generally sandblasted to a frosty texture.

Weinberg's work has evolved from rigid geometric compositions to organically arranged geometric forms that evoke the natural world. During this later phase the composition remains at the bottom of a mass of glass, and forms appear veiled due to the layers of glass that slump around the mold in the kiln. Veiled interior landscapes emerge from below, as if the viewer is being given a glimpse beneath the surface of the earth or sea (no. 71). In his *Untitled Pyramid* (no. 70), layers of glass suggest an erupting volcano. A brilliant bubble pulls elastic layers of glass upward against the force of gravity and is held in tense stasis within the peak of the pyramid.

Weinberg's astounding understanding of glass has allowed him a freedom to focus upon imagery. *Portrait of the "Doc" #1* pays tribute to Weinberg's father, who died in 1996. Mr. Weinberg studied death as a forensic pathologist—the mummies reference his career. Weinberg and his father enjoyed sport fishing together, hence the life-like bass fish and bobber. Fish have always symbolized creative force, and here the fish alludes to Weinberg, Sr.'s creative fantasies—or the big fish that never was caught. The dead whitefish head symbolizes Mr. Weinberg's Jewish heritage and love of food. Images from life are juxtaposed to images of death. Weinberg nearly titled this work, *He's My Hero*, but chose to avoid an idealized portrait. Vodka bottles imply that Weinberg's father was not superhuman, just a man who understood the fragility of life. Thus, Weinberg uses his mastery of the medium in the service of poetic expression. His willingness to take risks with narrative imagery, rather than trumpeting sensual, technical virtuosity, make him a significant artist in glass today.

LFN

Steven I. Weinberg
Portrait of the "Doc" #1, 1997 (no. 69)
Collection of the artist

Mary Ann ("Toots") Zynsky

In 1969 Toots Zynsky was attending high school in Lynnfield, Massachusetts. One day she decided to play hooky in order to pay a visit to the Museum of Fine Arts, Boston, when it was not too crowded. She spent the entire day in the galleries. The paintings never looked more wonderful; the colors were never more vibrant. Zynsky took off early on her love affair with art and color and adventure, and she is still flying. Today many of her creations, composed of thousands of threads of colored glass, all swirling in one direction, look as if they, too, are about to take flight.

A 1973 graduate of the Rhode Island School of Design, where she studied with Dale Chihuly (q.v.), Zynsky was extensively influenced by her later travels in South Africa, the Far East, and South America. Native textiles and wildlife, especially the plumage of birds, set her palette. In her first (1979) series of vessels she wound threads of glass around blown glass. She called these "dust collectors." In 1982 she began using her glass thread technique, arranging different colored filaments of glass in overlapping bundles. At first she pulled the threads by hand; later she used a machine developed for her by Mathijs Teunissen van Manen. The threads, pulled from rods of Murano glass 10 to 14 millimeters thick, are laid flat, one color on top of another, heated until they fuse, manipulated with spatulas, and slumped (or bent) in a stainless steel bowl or mold. The size, the rim contour, and above all the color vary markedly from piece to piece. *Brushfire* (1989), for example, is predominately brilliant acid oranges and a softer lime green, giving the impression that it is about to burst into flame. *Whitebird,* from the same year, is all white except for a few swirls of black and brown threads, and resembles a soft, graceful cup of feathers resting fleetingly on its journey in

space. Her creations speak to all the senses—some, with their jelly bean hues, look good enough to eat (*Blue, Green, and Lilac,* 1994); some evoke music, the movements of a symphony, the threads rising to a not quite finished crescendo (*Aquamarine,* 1990); while yet others, as in *Tierra del Fuego* (1988), with its primary colors, and *Red Chaos* (1994), its reds interspersed with black, speak impellingly to the erotic. *Chaos in Paradise* (no. 74) is from Zynsky's latest series in which she has stretched the bowl vertically to a taller vase form. The primary colors hark back to the Bird of Paradise series of 1990, but the extensive use of white threads produces a new fragility, while at the same time the colors seem to be fighting for prominence, hence the "chaos": which will reign supreme?

Zynsky, who works in Amsterdam, says she will "always consider Boston home." It is especially fitting, then, that her work is included in the current exhibition. A leading American studio glass artist, she has come a long way from the Pilchuck Glass School in Seattle, which she helped to found in 1971. Her work is in countless major museum and private collections in this country and abroad. While she did turn to drawing and pastels for a time, even ceasing to work in glass for five years (1974-79), she returned to it saying "Glass is such a strange and plastic thing—that's what draws me back to it."

ADM

Mary Ann ("Toots") Zynsky

Chaos in Paradise, 1995 (no. 74)

Collection of Dale and Doug Anderson

Checklist

Unless otherwise noted, dimensions are overall. Objects illustrated in the catalogue are indicated with an asterisk.

Howard Ben Tré
(b. 1949)

* 1. *Bench 8 and 9*
Pawtucket, Rhode Island, 1988
Cast solid glass, bronze, gold leaf, pigment, wax
H. 17 ½ in. W. 38 in. D. 17 in. (each)
Unmarked
Private collection

2. *Standing Column #37*
Pawtucket, Rhode Island, 1986
Cast solid glass, patinated brass, patinated copper, gold leaf, pigmented waxes
H. 96 in. W. 32 in. D. 12 in.
Unmarked
Museum of Fine Arts, Boston; gift of Dr. and Mrs. Joseph A. Chazan (1991.966)

Sonja Blomdahl
(b. 1952)

* 3. *Peach / Ruby / Cobalt*
Seattle, Washington, 1996
Blown glass
H. 16 ½ in. Diam. 13 in.
Signed: "Sonja / B8996"
Collection of the artist

4. *Pink / Clear / Blue*
Seattle, Washington, 1986
Blown glass
H. 8 ½ in. Diam. 12 ½ in.
Signed: "Sonja / SP1786"
Collection of the artist

5. *Cobalt / Chrome / Celadon*
Seattle, Washington, 1995
Blown glass
H. 21 ½ in. Diam. 14 in.
Signed: "Sonja B6995"
Collection of the artist

Dale Chihuly
(b. 1941)

6. *Navajo Blanket Cylinder*
Seattle, Washington, 1995
Blown glass
H. 18 in. Diam. 9 in.
Signed on bottom in orange hot glass: "DC / 95"
Collection of Dale and Doug Anderson

*7. *Blue Soft Cylinder with Green Lip Wrap*
Seattle, Washington, 1996
Blown glass
H. 17 in. W. 15 in. D. 17 in.
Signed on bottom: "Chihuly '96"
Collection of Dale and Doug Anderson

Carol Cohen
(b. 1939)

*8. *Greek Revival*
Cambridge, Massachusetts, 1994
Painted flat glass, painted wood
H. 24 in. W. 12 in. D. 11 in.
Engraved: "'Greek Revival' © 1994 Carol Cohen"
Museum of Fine Arts, Boston; Curator's Fund (1996.192)

9. *Little Compton*
Cambridge, Massachusetts, 1997
Painted flat glass, mixed media base
H. 60 in. W. 72 in. D. 18 in.
Engraved on bottom edge of layer one: "Little Compton © Carol Cohen"
Collection of the artist

10. *Fancy Slingbacks*
Cambridge, Massachusetts,1997
Painted flat glass, painted wood
H. 5 ½ in. W. 13 ½ in. D. 8 in.
Engraved on underside of layer one: "Fancy Slingbacks © 1997 Carol Cohen"
Collection of the artist

Dan Dailey
(b. 1947)

11. *Dancers with Dogs* (Circus Vase)
Seattle, Washington; Fenton, West Virginia; Kensington, New Hampshire, 1996
Blown, sandblasted, and acid-polished glass; patinated and gold-plated bronze
H. 27 ¾ in. Diam. 23 in.
Stamped: "Dailey CV 12-96"
Collection of the artist

12. *The Whirling Dervishes* (Circus Vase)
Seattle, Washington; Fenton, West Virginia; Kensington, New Hampshire, 1997
Blown, sandblasted and acid-polished glass; patinated and gold-plated bronze
H. 33 in. Diam. 16 in.
Stamped: "Dailey CV 15-97"
Collection of the artist

13. *Hippo*
Seattle, Washington; Fenton, West Virginia; Kensington, New Hampshire, 1994
Blown glass with hot-formed and applied features, sandblasted and acid-polished
H. 20 ½ in. Diam. 11 in.
Engraved on lower right edge of body: "Dan Dailey"; engraved on bottom: "AV 6-94"
Collection of the artist

*14. *Baboon*
Seattle, Washington; Fenton, West Virginia; Kensington, New Hampshire, 1994
Blown glass with hot-formed and applied features, sandblasted and acid-polished
H. 15 ½ in. W. 11 ½ in. D. 11 ½ in.
Engraved on edge: "Dailey"; engraved on bottom: "AV 25-94 / Baboon"
Collection of George and Dorothy Saxe

Michael M. Glancy
(b. 1950)

15. *Incognito Ruby Guardian*
Rehoboth, Massachusetts, 1988
Engraved blown glass, engraved blue industrial plate glass, copper, gold
H. 10 in. W. 10 in. D. 10 in.
Signed on base of vessel: "Michael Glancy Incognito Ruby Guardian"; signed on base: "Michael Glancy 1988"
Collection of Daniel Greenberg and Susan Steinhauser

*16. *UV Expansion*
Rehoboth, Massachusetts, 1994
Engraved blown glass, industrial plate glass, copper
H. 10 in. W. 21 in. D. 21 in.
Signed on base of vessel: "Michael Glancy 1994 UV Expansion"; signed on lower edge of base: "Michael Glancy 1994 UV Expansion"
Collection of Daniel Greenberg and Susan Steinhauser

17. *Magna Eclipsed*
Rehoboth, Massachusetts, 1986
Blown glass, industrial plate glass, copper, silver
H. 8 in. W. 25 in. D. 10 in.
Signed on base of vessel: "Michael Glancy 1986 Magna Eclipsed"; signed on lower edge of base: "Michael Glancy 1986 Magna Eclipsed"
Collection of Daniel Greenberg and Susan Steinhauser

Sidney R. Hutter
(b. 1954)

* 18. *Plate Glass Vase #28/08*
Waltham, Massachusetts, 1996
Laminated plate glass, cut, beveled, polished, with pink, orange, and yellow dyes
H. 16 ½ in. Diam. 10 ¾ in.
Signed on bottom: "Vase #28/08 / April 1996 / Sidney R. Hutter"
Museum of Fine Arts, Boston; gift of Samuel C. Crocker (1996.217)

19. *RA Quasi Modern #5*
Waltham, Massachusetts, 1997
Laminated, cut, and dyed plate glass
H. 18 in. Diam. 14 in.
Signed: "RA Quasi Modern / April 1997 / Sidney R. Hutter"
Collection of the artist

Kreg Kallenberger
(b. 1950)

* 20. *View at Saddleback Ridge*
from the Osage series
Tulsa, Oklahoma, 1990
Cast optical crystal, cut, polished, sandblasted, oil stained
H. 7 ⅜ in. W. 19 ½ in. D. 5 ½ in.
Signed: "K. Kallen 38790"
Museum of Fine Arts, Boston; this project was supported in part by a grant from the National Endowment for the Arts, a federal agency, and The Seminarians
(1990.122)

21. *Valley at Birch Creek*
Tulsa, Oklahoma, 1996
Cast optical crystal, cut, polished; stone
H. 18 ½ in. W. 12 in. D. 5 in.
Signed: "K. Kallen 55096"
Collection of Capital Resource Partners

Joey Kirkpatrick (b. 1952) and Flora C. Mace (b. 1949)

22. *The Conversation*
Seattle, Washington, 1983
Blown glass, copper wire, glass threads
H. 12 in. Diam. 8 in.
Etched in script on bottom: "Flora C. Mace Joey Kirkpatrick 1983"
Collection of Dale and Doug Anderson

* 23. *Still Life*
Seattle, Washington, 1997
Handblown glass, crushed glass colored powders, alderwood
H. (tallest piece) 31 in. Diam. base 57 in.
Diamond-scribed (each glass piece) in script: "Flora C. Mace Joey Kirkpatrick;" wood base signed: "Flora C. Mace Joey Kirkpatrick 1997"
Collection of the artists

Jon Kuhn
(b. 1949)

24. *CTVS #44*
Winston-Salem, North Carolina, 1980
Polished, chemically treated blown glass
H. 10 in. W. 6 in. D. 5 in.
Signed: "Jon Kuhn 1980 CTVS #44"
Collection of Dale and Doug Anderson

25. *Crystal Victory*
Winston-Salem, North Carolina, 1997
Optical lead crystal; optical borosilicate glass; fused, laminated, colored-glass powders
H. 9 ½ in. W. 9 ½ in. D. 9 ½ in.
Signed on bottom: "Jon Kuhn 1997 Crystal Victory"
Collection of the artist

* 26. *Desert Blush*
Winston-Salem, North Carolina, 1992
Optical lead crystal; optical borosilicate glass; fused, laminated, colored-glass powders
H. 24 in. W. 6 ½ in. D. 7 ½ in.
Signed on bottom: "Jon Kuhn 1992 Desert Blush"
Collection of the artist

Dominick Labino
(1910-1987)

* 27. *Emergence in Polychrome with Gold and Silver Veiling*
Grand Rapids, Ohio, 1970
Blown glass with mahogany base
H. 8 ½ in. W. 4 ¼ in. D. 2 ¼ in.
Signed on bottom: "Labino / 4-1970"
Museum of Fine Arts, Boston; gift of Mr. and Mrs. James A. Saks
(1983.294)

28. Vessel
Grand Rapids, Ohio, 1975
Core-formed and cased glass
H. 6 in. W. 2 ⅝ in. D. 2 ⅝ in.
Engraved on bottom: "Labino / 3-1975"
The Jones Museum of Glass and Ceramics

Marvin Lipofsky
(b. 1938)

With Stefan Stefko and team
* 29. *IGS III Series 1988-93 #4*
Novy Bor, Czechoslovakia, and Berkeley, California, 1988-93
Blown glass, sandblasted, ground, acid polished
H. 14 in. Diam. 23 in.
Signed: "IGS III #4"
Collection of the artist

With Unto Suominen
30. *Suomi Finland Series 1990-93 #11*
Suomi, Finland, and Berkeley, California, 1990-93
Blown glass, sandblasted, ground, acid polished
H. 11 ½ in. Diam. 16 in.
Signed: "Suomi Finland #11 1990-93"
Collection of the artist

Harvey K. Littleton
(b. 1922)

* 31. *Lemon / Red Crown*
Spruce Pine, North Carolina, 1989
Barium potash glass with multiple cased overlays of Kugler colors
H. 15 ¾ in. W. 34 in. D. 34 in.
Signed: "2-1989-5 Harvey Littleton"
Milwaukee Art Museum; gift of Peter and Grace Friend, Mr. and Mrs. Wayne J. Roper, Laurence and Judy Eiseman, Dr. and Mrs. Jurgen Herrmann, Dr. and Mrs. Leander Jennings, Nita Soref, Marilyn and Orren Bradley, Mr. and Mrs. Frank J. Pelisek, Dr. and Mrs. Robert Mann, Burton C. and Charlotte Zucker, James Brachman, Mr. and Mrs. John F. Monroe, Mr. and Mrs. Donald Wiiken, Elmer L. Winter, Mr. and Mrs. Stuart Goldfarb, Mr. Ben W. Heineman, Mr. and Mrs. Norman Hyman, Janey and Douglas MacNeil, and Friends (M1990.5)

Andrew Magdanz
(b. 1951)

* 32. Vessel
Cambridge, Massachusetts, 1997
Blown and cut soda-lime glass, colored lead glass
H. 32 in. Diam. 5 ¹³⁄₁₆ in.
Engraved on bottom: "Andrew Magdanz 1997"
Collection of the artist

33. Vessel
Cambridge, Massachusetts, 1997
Blown and cut soda-lime glass, colored lead glass
H. 19 in. Diam. 8 in.
Engraved on bottom: "Andrew Magdanz 1997"
Collection of the artist

34. Vessel
Cambridge, Massachusetts, 1997
Blown and cut soda-lime glass,
colored lead glass
H. 29 in. Diam. 9 ½ in.
Engraved on bottom: "Andrew
Magdanz 1997"
Collection of the artist

Dante Marioni
(b. 1964)

35. *Kelly Green Pair*
Seattle, Washington, 1996
Blown glass
H. (tallest piece) 38 ½ in.
Signed (each): "Marioni 1996"
Collection of Andrea and Charles
Bronfman

* 36. *Topaz Mosaic Vase*
Seattle, Washington, 1995
Blown glass
H. 34 ¾ in. Diam. 8 ½ in.
Signed: "Dante Marioni 1995
#7"
Collection of Andrea and Charles
Bronfman

Richard Marquis
(b. 1945)

37. *Checkerboard Teapot*
Langley, Washington, 1979
Blown glass, murrini decoration,
hot applications
H. 5 ¼ in. W. 5 ½ in. Diam. 4 ¾
in.
Signed: "M 028"
Collection of Dale and Doug
Anderson

38. *Marquiscarpa #38*
Langley, Washington, about 1992
Blown glass, murrini and battuto
techniques, fused, slumped, and
fabricated
H. 8 in. W. 12 ½ in. D. 3 ⅛ in.
Signed: "© Marquis"
Collection of Daniel Greenberg
and Susan Steinhauser

39. *Wizard Teapot*
Freeland, Washington, 1985
Blown glass, murrini canes (ani-
mals, stars, hearts), latticino cane
handle
H. 7 ½ in. Diam. 6 ¼ in.
Signed: "C.4.85 Marquis"
Collection of Daniel Greenberg
and Susan Steinhauser

* 40. *Cup with Toothbrush Feet*
Langley, Washington, 1980
Fabricated blown glass, plastic,
bristles
H. 8 in. W. 6 ⅛ in. D. 7 ½ in.
Unmarked
Collection of Susan Shapiro
Magdanz

**Richard Marquis and
Dante Marioni**

41. *Shard Whopper*
Seattle, Washington, 1992-95
Blown glass, glass shards
H. 29 in. Diam. 10 in.
Signed: "Marioni blown 1992,
Marquis decorated 1995"
Collection of Dale and Doug
Anderson

William Morris
(b. 1957)

* 42. *Canopic Jar: Big Horn
Sheep*
Stanwood, Washington, 1995
Blown glass
H. 24 in. Diam. 12 in.
Signed inside head: "William
Morris 1995"
Collection of Dale and Doug
Anderson

43. *Canopic Jar: Antelope*
Stanwood, Washington, 1995
Blown glass
H. 30 in. Diam. 9 in.
Signed inside head: "William
Morris 1995"
Collection of Dale and Doug
Anderson

44. *Suspended Artifact*
Stanwood, Washington, 1996
Blown glass
H. 33 in. W. 34 in. D. 9 in.
Signed on bottom of large urn:
"William Morris 1996"
Collection of Dale and Doug
Anderson

45. *Petroglyph V9516*
Stanwood, Washington, 1990
Blown glass
H. 23 ½ in. Diam. 22 in.
Signed on bottom: "William
Morris 1990"
Collection of Lorraine and Alan
Bressler

Jay Musler
(b. 1949)

46. *Five Goblets*
Berkeley, California, 1993
Blown Pyrex blanks
H. (tallest) 11 in. Diam. 5 ½ in.
Signed (each) on bottom:
"Musler / 93"
Collection of Dale and Doug
Anderson

* 47. *Mask House*
Berkeley, California, 1987
Plate glass, cut, sandblasted, and
painted
H. 30 in. W. 16 in. D. 7 in.
Signed on front of base: "Musler
87"
Collection of Dale and Doug
Anderson

48. *Cityscape*
Berkeley, California, 1986
Blown Pyrex blank, cut, sand-
blasted; airbrushed oil paint
H. 9 ⅛ in. Diam. 18 in.
Signed on bottom: "Musler 86"
Collection of Jeffrey and Cynthia
Manocherian

Joel Philip Myers
(b. 1934)

49. *Arctic Summer*
Bloomington, Illinois, 1990
Blown glass, colored glass shards
H. 15 ½ in. W. 15 ³⁄₁₆ in. D. 3 ⅞ in.
Engraved on side near bottom: "Joel
Philip Myers"
Collection of the artist

* 50. *Ørding Garden I*
Bloomington, Illinois, 1988
Blown glass, colored glass shards and
canes
H. 18 in. W. 21 in. D. 4 in.
Engraved on side near bottom: "Joel
Philip Myers"
Collection of Daniel Greenberg and
Susan Steinhauser

51. *Valmuen V*
Bloomington, Illinois, 1989
Blown glass, colored glass shards
H. 14 ⅞ in. W. 15 ⅞ in. D. 3 ¾ in.
Engraved on side near bottom: "Joel
Philip Myers"
Collection of Daniel Greenberg and
Susan Steinhauser

Thomas Patti
(b. 1943)

* 52. *Division of Fifty, Luminated
Particles for Doug*
Plainfield, Massachusetts, 1993
Fused, handshaped, ground, and pol-
ished glass
H. (tallest) 6 ⅜ in. W. (tallest) 5 ⅞ in.
Unmarked
Collection of Dale and Doug Anderson

53. *Red Echo with Blue*
Plainfield, Massachusetts, 1990
Fused, hand-shaped, ground, and pol-
ished glass
H. 3 ¹⁄₁₆ in. W. 6 ⁷⁄₁₆ in. D. 4 ½ in.
Signed on lower edge of side: "Patti
1990"
Collection of Linda J. Schwabe and
Stephen E. Elmont

54. *Spectral Gateway*
Plainfield, Massachusetts, 1997
Starphire float glass, fiber composite
H. (each) 109 in. W. (each) 40 in.
Signed on one panel: "© Patti 1997"
Collection of the artist

Ginny Ruffner
(b. 1952)

55. *What a Pear 2*
Seattle, Washington, 1996
Lampworked glass, paint, colored pencil
H. 26 in. W. 17 in. D. 18 in.
Signed on side: "Ginny Ruffner 96"
Collection of Dale and Doug Anderson

56. *Regarding Beauty* from the Conceptual Narrative series
Seattle, Washington, 1997
Lampworked glass, paint, colored pencil
H. 13 ¾ in. W. 13 ¾ in. D. 11 ½ in.
Signed: "Ginny Ruffner 97"
Collection of the artist

* 57. *What Is a Style?* from the Conceptual Narrative series
Seattle, Washington, 1997
Lampworked glass, paint, colored pencil
H. 13 in. W. 17 ½ in. D. 12 ½ in.
Signed: "Ginny Ruffner 97"
Collection of the artist

Mary Shaffer
(b. 1947)

58. *Red Hook*
Washington, D.C., 1996
Cast glass slumped on metal object
H. 26 in. W. 8 in. D. 7 in.
Signed on bottom left: "M. Shaffer 1996"
Collection of the artist

59. *Tool Wall*
Santa Fe, New Mexico, 1996-97
Slumped, plate, or cast glass on found metal and forged objects
H. (approx.) 8 ft. W. (approx.) 15 ft.
Engraved (each): "M. SHAFFER" and variant dates and numbers on individual pieces
Collection of the artist

* 60. *Wall Treasures II*
Washington, D.C., 1993
Glass, found objects, wire, graphite, wood
H. 28 in. W. 28 in. D. 7 in.
Unmarked
Collection of Simona and Jerome Chazen

Paul J. Stankard
(b. 1943)

61. *Forget Me Not with Root Spirit Block Botanical F46*
Mantua, New Jersey, 1990
Lampworked glass, crystal glass
H. 4 ¼ in. W. base 2 ¾ in.
Engraved: "Paul J. Stankard F46 1990"
Museum of Fine Arts, Boston; gift of George and Anna Krikorian and our son, George (1990.485)

* 62. *Golden Bowl Diptych*
Mantua, New Jersey, 1996
Lampworked glass, crystal glass
H. 5 ¾ in. W. 5 ⅛ in. D. 2 ½ in.
Engraved: "Paul J. Stankard D8 '96"
Collection of Lois Sandler

63. *Goatsbeard Daisy Bouquet Cloistered Botanical*
Mantua, New Jersey, 1989
Lampworked glass, crystal glass
H. 6 ½ in.
Engraved: "Paul J. Stankard F19"
Collection of Mike and Annie Belkin

64. *Yellow Goatsbeard with Spirits Cloistered Botanical*
Mantua, New Jersey, 1989
Lampworked glass, crystal glass
H. 6 ¾ in. W. 3 ¼ in. D. 3 in.
Engraved on reverse: "Paul J. Stankard F39 1989"
Collection of Dale and Doug Anderson

Catherine ("Cappy") Thompson
(b. 1952)

65. *Searching for the Bodhisattva: A Spirit Canoe Carries My Soul Toward the Divine Child of My Dreams*
Seattle, Washington, 1996
Vitreous enamels on blown glass, reverse painted
H. 21 in. Diam. 11 ½ in.
Signed: "Searching for the Bodhisattva: A Spirit Canoe Carries My Soul Toward the Divine Child of My Dreams/Cappy Thompson/ 1996"
Collection of the artist

* 66. *Fiddler*
Seattle, Washington, 1991
Vitreous enamels on blown glass, reverse painted
H. 23 in. Diam. 14 in.
Signed: "Fiddler 1991"
Collection of Simona and Jerome Chazen

Karla Trinkley
(b. 1956)

67. *Birdboat*
Boyertown, Pennsylvania, 1994
Cast glass *(pâte de verre)*, poplar and cedar coated with graphite, metal
H. 25 in. W. 36 in. D. 12 ¼ in.
Unmarked
Collection of Daniel Greenberg and Susan Steinhauser

* 68. *Terrapene*
Boyertown, Pennsylvania, 1994
Cast glass *(pâte de verre)*
H. 13 in. Diam. 21 in.
Unmarked
Collection of the artist

Steven I. Weinberg
(b. 1954)

* 69. *Portrait of the "Doc" #1*
Pawtucket, Rhode Island, 1997
Cast crystal glass, granite base
H. 12 in. W. 9 in. D. 9 ½ in.
Signed: "#790201 Steven Weinberg"
Collection of the artist

70. *Untitled pyramid*
Pawtucket, Rhode Island, 1996
Cast crystal
H. 7 ½ in. W. 8 ½ in. D. 8 ½ in.
Signed: "Weinberg PYR 08/95"
Collection of the artist

71. *Untitled cube*
Pawtucket, Rhode Island, 1991
Cast, slumped crystal glass
H. 9 in. W. 9 in. D. 9 in.
Marked: "Weinberg 191101"
Collection of Judy and Robbie Mann

Mary Ann ("Toots") Zynsky
(b. 1951)

72. *Extra Golden Chaos*
Amsterdam, The Netherlands, 1996
Fused glass fibers
H. 12 ¼ in. W. 19 ¼ in. D. 15 ½ in.
Signed: "Z"
Collection of Alfred DeCredico

73. *Bird of Paradise*
Amsterdam, The Netherlands, 1987
Fused glass fibers
H. 5 ½ in. Diam. 12 in.
Signed: "Z"
Collection of Dale and Doug Anderson

* 74. *Chaos in Paradise*
Amsterdam, The Netherlands, 1995
Fused glass fibers
H. 7 in. W. 14 in.
Signed: "Z"
Collection of Dale and Doug Anderson

A Brief Glossary of Glassmaking Terms and Techniques

Human imagination and the discovery of the physics of sight and light are inextricably linked to the ductile but seemingly solid noncrystalline material called glass. This is an artificial, man-made substance compounded as early as western civilization's beginnings around 3000 B.C. Although there exist thousands of different formulae for glassmaking, a representative batch of soda-lime glass might consist of sand (65 percent silica), soda ash (20 percent sodium oxide), and lime (15 percent calcium oxide). Substitution of lead oxide for calcium oxide produces a brilliant, "flint" glass that has the appearance of quartz-like crystal. Few materials made by mankind seem more precious or are as visually seductive as glass, yet at the same time few materials are processed in such large quantities so as to be taken for granted in modern society.

Glass is a medium almost unique in the ability it has given mankind to unravel the mysteries of light and color. Without glass it would be difficult to explore how light travels, how it is reflected, refracted, or bent into a rainbow of prismatic hues. The glass of lenses and of mirrors plays a primary role in probing distant luminous bodies in the heavens and inspecting the smallest particles on earth. The importance of glass for lenses in photography and use in eyeglasses seems almost too obvious to mention. Glass also forms an important material of everyday use in windows, tablewares, building blocks, insulation, fiberglass ropes, and molding media for auto and boat bodies. Glass also continues to dazzle the eye in fashionable wearing apparel, jewelry, crystal sconces, goblets, and chandeliers. Little wonder, then, that glass holds extraordinary appeal to artists who grasp its potential as an expressive medium.

Glass does not have a precise melting point; it simply becomes more liquid with higher temperatures. Most glassworking requires teamwork to handle the hot glass medium. It can be worked either hot or cold. In a hot, viscous state, it is blown, pressed into molds, cast, fused, laminated, slumped, colored, and otherwise manipulated. Cold, it is cut, acid etched, sandblasted, ground, polished, sawn, electroplated, chiseled, epoxied, enameled, stained, and otherwise painted. All such treatments, in differing combinations, are to be found employed in the making of the glass works of art included in this exhibition.

A delight and sometimes a puzzle to the eye of the viewer results from this wide spectrum of working methods. But technique is not an end in itself. In the hands of gifted artists, technique is a means by which artistic problems are explored. Glass has its own demands that cannot be ignored by the artist. Until fairly recently, the knowledge and equipment necessary to make the medium accessible to the studio artist was kept a carefully guarded trade secret.

The following definitions provide a brief introduction to various techniques and terms. Each artist practices the craft in idiosyncratic ways too various to be summarized here. For more detailed information, see Harold Newman, *An Illustrated Dictionary of Glass* (New York: Thames and Hudson, 1977); Charles Bray, *Dictionary of Glass: Materials and Techniques* (London: A. & C. Black; Philadelphia: University of Pennsylvania Press, 1995), which is aimed more specifically at modern studio glass and commercial techniques; and Peter Layton, *Glass Art* (London: A. and C. Black; Seattle, Wash.: University of Washington Press, 1996), especially the section on "Materials and Techniques," pp. 106-95. Early techniques are covered in David Frederick Grose, *Early Ancient Glass* (New York: Hudson Hills Press in association with the Toledo Museum of Art, 1989).

JLF & GWRW

Acid-etching: The process of using hydrofluoric acid in combination with stencils or resists, to produce decorative designs by cutting or eating away the glass.

Annealing: Cooling molten glass, over substantial periods of time, to avoid the damaging effects of stress.

Blown (or free-blown) glass: Glass produced by the traditional process of rolling a molten gather of glass on a flat surface or *marver,* and blowing air through a metal tube or blow-pipe into it.

Cast: Glass produced by the kiln-casting *Cire perdue* (lost wax) method or by sand casting (pouring hot glass into a mold).

Cold work: General term embracing techniques that do not involve hot glass, such as cutting, etching, polishing, sandblasting, and laminating.

Constructed: Objects made by the combination of glass (and other materials) glued, epoxied, fused, bolted, or otherwise joined together.

Cut glass: Glass decorated through wheel-cut designs.

Electroforming or electroplating: The electrochemical application of a thin layer of metal to a glass surface.

Engraving: Abrading the surface of glass with a copper, diamond, or other wheel, or stippling the surface with a diamond-point tool; modern makers also embrace the terms *etching* and *sandblasting* under this rubric.

Epoxy resin: A synthetic resin used to bond glass in laminated or sculptural constructions.

Flamework: see Lampwork.

Fusing: Heating pieces of glass until they bond.

Gaffer: The lead or chief glassblower.

Gather: A gob of molten glass.

Iridescence: The surface rainbow of colors achieved by coating glass with a thin metallic or other layer.

Lamination: The process of gluing together layers of sheet or plate glass, and/or bonding them with resin, which can then be additionally worked as an assemblage.

Lampwork: A technique of working tubular glass rods at a bench by heating with a small flame, generally today a gas blowtorch, and manipulating with tongs, forceps, knives, and other small tools, often handmade. Also called flamework.

Marver: A flat surface, originally of marble but now of stainless steel, used for rolling gathers.

Millefiori: An Italian term (a thousand flowers) used to describe glass decorated with slices of colored canes embedded in clear molten glass, usually in flowerlike designs.

Murrini: An Italian term for a form of modern mosaic glass distinguished by large pieces or streaks of varied color glass, as opposed to the more geometric, embedded designs found in canes of millefiori glass.

Parison (or paraison): The initial gather of glass, shaped and blown into a bubble for working.

Pâte de verre: A paste of ground or crushed glass, and the technique of casting this material into a mold; also applied to a more general range of cast-glass objects.

Pontil (or punty): A steel rod or tube used in the blowing process.

Pressed glass: Glass produced by pressing the material with a plunger into a mold.

Sandblasting: The use of compressed air to project abrasive materials, originally sand but now more likely aluminum oxide or silicon carbide, against glass to create a matte surface or to penetrate the object.

Sawing: Cutting and shaping glass with a diamond blade fitted to a mechanized saw.

Slumping: The technique of heating glass until it falls or drops into a desired shape as configured by a mold or supporting framework; also referred to as sagging when a mold is not used.

Selected Bibliography

The following list primarily includes titles pertaining to studio glass since the 1960s; a few general works on the history of American glass as a whole are also represented. Several works pertinent to the discussion of each contemporary artist's work in the exhibition are also included. For a guide to the literature on early American glass, see Kirk J. Nelson, "American Glass," in Kenneth L. Ames and Gerald W.R. Ward, eds., *Decorative Arts and Household Furnishings in America, 1650-1920: An Annotated Bibliography* (Winterthur, Del.: Henry Francis du Pont Winterthur Museum, 1989), pp. 221-35. GWRW

The Art of Painted Glass. Boca Raton, Fla.: Habatat Gallery, 1995.

Beard, Geoffrey. *International Modern Glass.* New York: Charles Scribner's Sons, 1976.

Biskeborn, Susan. *Artists at Work: Twenty-five Glassmakers, Ceramists, and Jewelers.* Seattle, Wash., and Anchorage, Alaska: Alaska Northwest Books, 1990.

Bray, Charles. *Dictionary of Glass: Materials and Techniques.* London: A.C. Black; Philadelphia: University of Pennsylvania Press, 1995.

Charleston, Robert J. *Masterpieces of Glass: A World History from the Corning Museum of Glass.* New York: Harry N. Abrams, 1990.

Contemporary Glass: A Private Collection. N.p.: Falcon II Press, 1988.

Contemporary Glass: The Collection of Jean and Hilbert Sosin: Twenty-five Years of Studio Glass, March 23, 1962, to March 23, 1987. Dearborn, Mich.: University of Michigan-Dearborn, 1987.

Contemporary Glass: The Sam and Beverly Ross Collection. St. Petersburg, Fla.: Museum of Fine Arts, St. Petersburg, 1989.

Cooke, Frederick. *Glass: Twentieth-Century Design.* New York: E.P. Dutton, 1986.

Corning Museum of Glass. *Glass 1959: A Special Exhibition of Contemporary Glass.* Corning, N.Y.: By the museum, 1959.

Corning Museum of Glass. *New Glass: A Worldwide Survey.* Corning, N.Y.: By the museum, 1979.

Craft Today USA. New York: American Craft Museum, 1989.

Frantz, Susanne K. *Contemporary Glass: A World Survey from the Corning Museum of Glass.* New York: Harry N. Abrams, 1989.

Glass Routes. Lincoln, Mass.: DeCordova Museum, 1981.

Grover, Ray, and Lee Grover. *Contemporary Art Glass.* New York: Crown, 1975.

Herman, Lloyd E., with an introduction by Dale Chihuly. *Clearly Art: Pilchuck's Glass Legacy.* Bellingham, Wash.: Whatcom Museum of History and Art, 1992.

Hessel, Patricia Moore. *Glass and Clay: The Leight Collection.* Lexington, Ken.: J.B. Speed Art Museum, 1984.

Klein, Dan. *Glass: A Contemporary Art.* New York: Rizzoli, 1989.

Layton, Peter. *Glass Art.* London: A.C. Black; Seattle: University of Washington Press, 1996.

Lipofsky, Marvin. *Breaking Traditions: Contemporary Artists Who Use Glass.* Danville, Cal.: University of California at Berkeley Museum at Blackhawk, 1994.

Manhart, Marcia, Tom Manhart, and Carol Haralson, eds. *The Eloquent Object: The Evolution of American Art in Craft Media Since 1945.* Tulsa, Okla.: Philbrook Museum of Art, 1987.

Mentasti, Rosa Barovier. *Venetian Glass, 1890-1990.* Venice: Arsenale Editrice, 1992.

Merrill, Nancy O. *A Concise History of Glass Represented in the Chrysler Museum Glass Collection.* Norfolk, Va.: By the museum, 1989.

Miller, Bonnie J. *Out of the Fire: Contemporary Glass Artists and Their Work.* San Francisco: Chronicle Books, 1991.

Monroe, Michael W., with an essay by Barbaralee Diamonstein. *The White House Collection of American Crafts.* New York: Harry N. Abrams, 1995.

National Museum of Modern Art, Kyoto, ed. *Contemporary Studio Glass: An International Collection.* Kyoto, Japan: By the museum, 1982.

Oldknow, Tina. *Pilchuck: A Glass School.* Seattle, Wash.: Pilchuk Glass School in association with the University of Washington Press, 1996.

Ruffner, Ginny, Ron Glowen, and Kim Levin. *Glass: Material in the Service of Meaning.* Tacoma, Wash.: Tacoma Art Museum in association with University of Washington Press, 1992.

Sarpellon, Giovanni. *Lino Tagliapietra: Glass.* Venice: Arsenale Editrice, 1994.

Smith, Paul J., and Edward Lucie-Smith. *Craft Today: Poetry of the Physical: American Craft Museum.* New York: Weidenfeld & Nicholson, 1986.

Spillman, Jane Shadel, and Susanne K. Frantz. *Masterpieces of American Glass: The Corning Museum of Glass, The Toledo Museum of Art, Lillian Nassau Ltd.* New York: Crown, 1990.

Studio Glass in the Metropolitan Museum of Art. Introduction by Jane Adlin. New York: By the museum, 1996.

Taragin, Davira S., et al. *Contemporary Crafts and the Saxe Collection.* New York: Hudson Hills Press and the Toledo Museum of Art, 1993.

Waldrich, Joachim. *Who's Who in Contemporary Glass: A Comprehensive World Guide to Glass Artists, Craftsmen, Designers.* Munich: J. Waldrich Verlag, 1993.

Warmus, William. *The Venetians: Modern Glass, 1919-1990.* New York: Muriel Karasik Gallery, 1989.

World Glass Now '88. Sapporo, Japan: Hokkaido Museum of Modern Art, 1988.

Zerwick, Chloe. *A Short History of Glass.* Corning, N.Y.: Corning Museum of Glass, 1980.

Artists in the Exhibition

The artists in this exhibition are discussed in many of the general works cited above. Copious documentation on each maker, including videotapes in many instances, is contained in the maker's files in the Department of American Decorative Arts and Sculpture. The following monographs provide an introduction to the evolving work of each person.

Ben Tré, Howard

Howard Ben Tré: Basins. Farmington Hills, Mich.: Habatat Galleries, 1992.

Howard Ben Tré: Basins and Fountains. Kingston, R.I.: Fine Arts Center Galleries, University of Rhode Island, 1994.

Howard Ben Tré: Recent Sculpture. Richmond, Va.: Marsh Art Gallery, University of Richmond, in association with the Cleveland Center for Contemporary Art, 1995.

Kangas, Matthew. "Engendering Ben Tré." *Glass Magazine,* no. 40 (Spring/Summer 1990): 20-27.

Onorato, Ronald J. "Howard Ben Tré." *Art New England* 11, no. 10 (November 1990): 18-19, 32.

Blomdahl, Sonja

Kaplos, Janet. "Matters of Mood: The Glass of Sonja Blomdahl." *Glass Magazine,* no. 59 (Spring 1995): 34-41.

Chihuly, Dale

Bannard, Walter Bannard, and Henry Geldzahler. *Chihuly: Form from Fire.* Daytona Beach, Fla.: Museum of Arts and Sciences, Inc., Daytona Beach, in association with University of Washington Press, 1993.

Bremser, Sarah E. *Chihuly Courtyards.* Honolulu: Honolulu Academy of Arts, 1995.

Chihuly, Dale. *Chihuly: Color, Glass, and Form.* New York: Kodansha International/USA Ltd., 1986.

Chihuly Baskets. Introduction by Linda Norden. Seattle, Wash.: Portland Press, 1996.

Chihuly Over Venice. Text by William Warmus and Dana Self. Seattle, Wash.: Portland Press, 1996.

Chihuly Seaforms. Introduction by Sylvia Earle. Seattle, Wash.: Portland Press, 1995.

Cowart, Jack, and Karen Chambers. *Chihuly: A Decade of Glass.* Bellevue, Wash.: Bellevue Art Museum, 1984.

Dale Chihuly Glass. Introduction by Linda Norden. N.p.: 1982.

Dale Chihuly: objets de verre. Paris: Musée des Arts Décoratifs, 1986.

Geldzahler, Henry. *Chihuly/Persians.* Bridgehampton, N.Y.: Dia Art Foundation, 1988.

Glowen, Ron, and Dale Chihuly. *Venetians: Dale Chihuly.* Altadena, Calif.: Twin Palms Publishers, 1989.

Hobbs, Robert. *Chihuly alla Macchia from the George R. Stroemple Collection.* Beaumont, Tex.: Art Museum of Southeast Texas, 1993.

Sims, Patterson. *Dale Chihuly: Installations 1964-1992.* Seattle: Seattle Art Museum, 1992.

Cohen, Carol

Hollister, Paul. "Jon Kuhn and Carol Cohen: Exploration of Inner Space." *Neues Glas* (October/December 1988): 283-87.

"Interview: Carol Cohen." *Glass Focus* (The Official Newsletter of the Art Alliance for Contemporary Glass) 9 (February/March 1995): 1, 15-17.

Dailey, Dan

Chambers, Karen. "Dan Dailey: A Designing Character." *Neues Glas* (January/February/March 1990): 10-19.

"Dan Dailey: Captured Phenomena." *New Work.* New York: New York Experimental Glass Workshop, [ca. 1979].

"Dan Dailey: Directions in Glass." *American Craft* 41, no. 1 (February/March 1981): 24-27, 75-76.

Dan Dailey: Simple Complexities in Drawings and Glass, 1972-1987. Philadelphia: Rosenwald-Wolf Gallery, Philadelphia Colleges of the Arts, 1987.

Matano, Koji. "Dan Dailey." *Glasswork* 6 (August 1990): 12-19.

Glancy, Michael M.

Constellations: An Alternative Galaxy: Glass by Michael Glancy. With contributions by Miklos von Bartha, Dan Klein, Dale Chihuly, and Erik Gottschalk. [Basil, Switzerland]: Edition von Bartha, [1995].

McTwigan, Michael. "Michael Glancy: Balancing Order and Chaos." *Glass Magazine,* no. 42 (Winter 1990): 22-29.

Michael Glancy/June 1989. Foreword by Lisa Hammel. N.p.: 1989.

Hutter, Sidney R.

Waggoner, Shawn. "On the Cutting Edge: Sidney Hutter's Laminated Glass Sculpture." *Glass Art* 11, no. 5 (July/August 1996): 4-11.

Kallenberger, Kreg

Heinsen, Lindsay. "The Southern Artist: Kreg Kallenberger." *Southern Accents* 14, no. 1 (February 1991): 86-89.

Kallenberger: 3 Series in Glass. Tulsa, Okla.: Philbrook Art Center, [1986].

Kirkpatrick, Joey, and Mace, Flora C.

Kirkpatrick/Mace: April 15-August 15, 1993. Ames, Iowa: Brunnier Gallery and Museum, Iowa State Museum, 1993.

Miller, Bonnie. "Double Vision." *American Craft* 49, no. 5 (October 1989): 40-45.

Kuhn, Jon

Byrd, Joan Falconer. "Jon Kuhn: Radiant Vision." *American Craft* 55, no. 5 (October/November 1995): 70-73.

Jon Kuhn. Farmington Hills, Mich., and Boca Raton, Fla.: Habatat Galleries, 1992.

Jon Kuhn, December 7-January 6, 1996. Boca Raton, Fla.: Habatat Galleries, 1995.

Jon Kuhn, December 12 to January 4, 1997. Boca Raton, Fla.: Habatat Galleries, 1996.

Jon Kuhn: Glass. Traverse City, Mich.: Dennos Museum Center, Northwestern Michigan College, 1993.

Labino, Dominick

Dominick Labino: A Decade of Glass Craftsmanship, 1964-1974. Toledo, Ohio: Pilkington Glass Museum, Victoria and Albert Museum, Toledo Museum of Art, 1974.

Labino, Dominick. "The Egyptian Sand-Core Technique: A New Interpretation." *Journal of Glass Studies* 8 (1966): 124-27.

Labino, Dominick. *Visual Art in Glass.* Dubuque, Iowa: William C. Brown Co., 1968.

Lipofsky, Marvin

Marvin Lipofsky: Pilchuck Series, 1984-1985. Palm Beach, Fla.: Holsten Galleries, 1985.

White, Cheryl. "Marvin Lipofsky: Roving Ambassador of Glass." *American Craft* 51, no. 5 (October/November 1991): 46-51.

Littleton, Harvey K.

Byrd, Joan Falconer. *Harvey K. Littleton: A Retrospective Exhibition.* Atlanta, Ga.: High Museum of Art, 1984.

Littleton, Harvey K. *Glassblowing: A Search for Form.* New York: Van Nostrand Reinhold Co., 1971.

Magdanz, Andrew

Lamar, Michael. "Boston Diary." *New Work,* no. 35 (Fall 1988): 8-17.

"Shaping a Career in Glass Design." *Boston Globe* (June 18, 1987).

Marioni, Dante

Brunsman, Laura A. "Dante Marioni." *Glass Magazine,* no. 49 (Fall 1992): 52.

Kangas, Matthew. "Dante Marioni: Apprentice to Tradition." *American Craft* 54, no. 1 (February-March 1994): 34-37.

Marquis, Richard

Marquis, Richard. "murrini/canne." *Glass Art Magazine* 1, no. 1 (January-February 1973): 39-44.

Matano, Koji. "Richard Marquis." *Glasswork* 2 (July 1989): 20-25.

Miller, Bonnie. "The Irreverent Mr. Marquis." *Neues Glas* (April/June 1988): 78-84.

Porges, Maria. "Richard Marquis, Material Culture." *American Craft* 55, no. 1 (December 1995/January 1996): 36-38, 62.

Taylor, Gay LeCleire. *Thousands of Flowers: American Millefiori Glass.* Millville, N.J.: Museum of American Glass at Wheaton Village, 1992.

Morris, William

Blonston, Gary. *William Morris: Artifacts/Glass.* New York: Abbeville Press, 1996.

Geldzahler, Henry, and Patterson Sims. *William Morris, Glass: Artifact and Art.* Seattle and London: University of Washington Press, 1989.

Musler, Jay

Hammel, Lisa. "An Apocalyptic Art." *American Craft* 48, no. 5 (October/November 1988): 26-31.

Hollister, Paul. "Jay Musler's Painted Glass: The Face of Anger." *Neues Glas* (January/February/March 1985): 12-19.

Marks, Ben. "The Brinksmanship of Jay Musler." *Glass Magazine,* no. 49 (Fall 1992): 20-25.

Myers, Joel Philip

Boylen, Michael. "Compositions on Black: Joel Philip Myers." *American Craft* 40, no. 5 (October/November 1980): 8-11.

Hollister, Paul. "Joel Philip Myers' Glass: 'A Quiet, Peaceful Way of Working.'" *Neues Glas* (July/ September 1983): 128-33.

Joel Philip Myers. Los Angeles: Kurland/Summers Gallery, 1988.

Joel Philip Myers' Exhibition. Ebeltoft, Denmark: Glasmuseum, 1993.

Joel Philip Myers: Oeuvres. Introduction by Dan Klein. Paris: Clara Scremini Gallery, 1988.

Myers, Joel. "Joel Myers and Blenko Glass." *Craft Horizons* 24, no. 2 (March/April 1964): 36-37.

Patti, Thomas

Goldstein, Sidney M. *Currents 24: Tom Patti.* St. Louis: St. Louis Art Museum, 1984.

Hollister, Paul. "Monumentality in Miniature." *American Craft* 43, no. 3 (June/July 1983): 14-18, 88.

Hollister, Paul. "Tom Patti: The Code Is in the Glass." *Neues Glas* (April/June 1983): 74-83.

Thomas Patti: Azurlites, 1991-1993. Paris: Galerie Internationale Du Verre, 1993.

Tom Patti: Glass. Text by Robert Henning, Jr. Springfield, Mass.: George Walter Vincent Smith Art Museum, 1980.

Ruffner, Ginny

Bock, Paula. "Mind Over Matter: The Amazing Brain of Ginny Ruffner." *The Seattle Times* (July 16, 1995).

Kangas, Matthew. "Unravelling Ruffner. *Glass Magazine,* no. 43 (Spring 1991): 20-29.

Miller, Bonnie J. *Why Not? The Art of Ginny Ruffner.* Seattle and London: Tacoma Art Museum in association with the University of Washington Press, 1995.

Waggoner, Shawn. "With Visibility Comes Greater Responsibility: A Conversation with Ginny Ruffner." *Glass Art* 7, no. 2 (January/February 1992): 4-8.

Yood, James. "Ruffner and Kursh." *Glass Magazine,* no. 60 (Fall 1995): 28-33.

Shaffer, Mary

Diamonstein, Barbaralee. *Handmade in America: Conversations with Fourteen Craftmasters.* New York: Harry N. Abrams, 1983, pp. 216-23.

Mary Shaffer. Farmington Hills, Mich.: Habatat Galleries, 1992.

Mary Shaffer. Farmington Hills, Mich.: Habatat Galleries, 1994.

Waggoner, Shawn. "Your Art is What You Are." *Glass Art* 5, no. 3 (March/April 1990): 62-66.

Stankard, Paul J.

Dietz, Ulysses Grant. *Paul J. Stankard: Homage to Nature.* New York: Harry N. Abrams, 1996.

Hollister, Paul. "Natural Wonders: The Lampwork of Paul J. Stankard." *American Craft* 47, no. 1 (February/March 1987): 36-43.

Thompson, Catherine ("Cappy")

Glowen, Ron. "Cappy Thompson's Fabled World." *Glass Magazine,* no. 47 (Spring 1992): 20-27.

Waggoner, Shawn. "Cappy Thompson: Narrative, Mythopoesis, and the Vessel Form." *Glass Art* 12, no. 1 (January/February): 4-9.

Trinkley, Karla

Miller, Bonnie J. "Karla Trinkley: Silent Spaces." *New Work,* no. 31 (Fall 1987): 24-25.

Weinberg, Steven I.

Hollister, Paul. "Steven Weinberg's Casting Technique Something New under the Sun." *Neues Glas* (January/February/March 1981): 143-47.

Steven I. Weinberg: Concatenation. Providence, R.I.: Industrial Impressions, 1983.

Zynsky, Mary Ann ("Toots")

Jaulin, Aline, Linda Norden, and Nane Stern. *Toots Zynsky: Oeuvres.* Paris: Clara Scremini Gallery, 1987.

Olivié, Jean Luc, and Jean-Pascal Billaud. *Toots Zynsky.* Paris: Clara Scremini Gallery, 1990.

Sinz, Dagmar. "Toots Zynsky: Color for Color." *Neues Glas* (October/December 1987): 276-79.

Waggoner, Shawn. "My Full Name is Mary Ann Toots Zynsky. But Toots Just Suites [*sic*] Me Better I Guess." *Glass Art* 4, no. 5 (July/August 1989): 86-89.